Before Lunch

'Emerging from the voices of absent people, between their pictured possibilities, memories and fears, the London visitor and her country hostess talk, the one's regular beat counterpointed by the other's *vers libre*.' – Vyvian Jones

VAL WARNER

Before Lunch

CARCANET

For Jennifer Birkett

First published in 1986 by
Carcanet Press Limited
208-212 Corn Exchange Buildings
Manchester M4 3BQ

All rights reserved

Copyright © Val Warner 1986

British Library Cataloguing in Publication Data
Warner, Val
 Before Lunch.
 I. Title
 821'.914   PR6073.A729

ISBN 0-85635-629-8

The Publisher acknowledges financial assistance
from the Arts Council of Great Britain

Typeset by Bryan Williamson, Swinton, Berwickshire
Printed in England by SRP Ltd., Exeter

Contents

Leaving the Second-hand Bookshop	9
Cleaner	14
Pie in the Sky	17
A.I. in Paris	18
Rosemary's Baby	19
Sub-standard	20
Rejection, the Literary Life	21
A Version of Tristan	22
Black and White	23
Onions and Tulips	23
The Rotted House	24
1. Ground of Our Being	24
2. Twilight Zone	25
3. Scene of the Crime	25
4. The Rotted House	26
5. Missing the Bus?	26
6. Summer of 72	27
7. Fustian	27
8. Jim's Legacy	28
9. Nature, Nurture	29
10. On the Balcony, Next Door	29
11. Talking to Yourself?	30
12. Moorgate, Passing on	30
13. Correspondence	31
14. Gossiping over Lady Diana Cooper's Memoirs	31
15. Snap-shots	32
16. "Let This Cup Pass from Me"	33
17. Dust	33
Circumscribed	34
Derelict Landlord	35
1. Derelict Landlord	35
2. Restoration	36
The Picture in the Picture	38
In the Picture	38
In the Cage	39
Humanities' Computing Course (1979)	40

Dandelion	45
After the Programme	46
Drawing the Curtain	49
Ann, Intimations	50
In the Green-house	51
For ever Amber	52
Thin Red Line	53
Woman with Green Eyes	53
Never Such Light	56
1. Never Such Light	56
2. In Love	57
3. May We See	60
4. Copper Beech	61
5. Dead Moths	61
6. Moonlight and Thistles	63
7. Pathetic Fallacy	64
Other Men's Flowers	64
Northern Ireland Peace March, London	65
Going Home	74
1. Across the Yard	74
2. By Half-light	74
3. Going Home ("Soon, winter…")	75
The Rose, the Hearth	76
1. Corned-beef Legs	76
2. The Rose, the Hearth	77
Remembered Melon	77
Tied Home	78
1. Tied Home	78
2. Tied Home	79
3. Tied Home	79
4. Farm Cottage to View, near Gauldry	80
5. Farm Cottage to View, near Gauldry	80
6. Electric Storm	81
7. Going Home ("In the outsider's…")	81
8. Setting the World on Fire	82
9. Poor Tom's	82
10. From the Window-seat	83
Freeze	84

Days of Grace	84
Warp	85
Talking to Yourself	86
A Good Listener	87
A Privileged Voice	87
Woman with a Mandolin	88
Portrait of a Lady	89
Weedy Plot	90
Reader's Friend	90
Last Tango in Paisley	91
Sub Rosa	93
Ann, before Lunch	93
By St Paul's Parish Church, Sketty	97
House on Mumbles Road	98
At the Hearth	101
Iron in the Soul	103
Pre-publication?	106
White Trash	107
Free Speech	108
House Arrest	108
Letters	109
1. The Snowplough	109
2. Letters ("No news…")	110
3. Hospital	111
4. Mourning	111
5. Local Anaesthetic	112
In G Minor	113
At the Lights	114
Collusion	114
Rape	115
Letters ("This mild night…")	116
Silver-fish	117
"The Realms of Gold"	118
In the 70s	118
1. In the 70s	118
2. End of Another Bank Holiday	120
Tomorrow	122
Sprout	126

Soil	127
Street Collection (1979)	128
Workcamp	130

Acknowledgements and thanks are due to the editors of the following magazines and anthologies where some of these poems have previously appeared, occasionally with different titles and often in other versions: *Acumen, Ambit, AMF, Antaeus* (USA), *Bananas, Blind Serpent, British Poetry since 1970* (Carcanet), *Caret, Chapman, Cracked Looking Glass, Critical Quarterly, Encounter, Folio International, Gairfish, Gallimaufry, Green River Review* (USA), *The Honest Ulsterman, Lines Review, Madog, Meridian, New Poetry 1* and *3* (Arts Council of Great Britain), *Ostrich, Other Poetry, Outposts, PN Review, Penny Poems, Pequod* (USA), *Pick, Poems 85,* (Lancaster Literature Festival), *Poems for Shakespeare IV* (The Globe Playhouse Trust), *Poetry Durham, Poetry Review, Poetry Wales, The Scotsman, Seagate II* (Taxus Press), *Verse, Vision On, Young Winter's Tales 6* and *8* (Macmillan).

Some poems have been broadcast by the BBC, Radio 3. Some were included in *Writers in Brief 12: Val Warner* (National Book League, Glasgow, 1980). One poem was published as a Ram card (London, 1979). Four poems were included in an unfinished sequence which won a Gregory Award.

I should like to thank Anthony Rudolf for reading the typescript and Jill Farringdon for commenting on some of the poems, and also Krishna and Utpal Ghosh and Brenda Shaw for other help.

Leaving the Second-hand Bookshop

With a final flutter
of two green notes, I leaf
between branchy towers
of his eye-lashes. The bookseller
tots up change. Is giving
so little for so much
immoral? Silver and bronze
stream into the skull

of my cupped hand. Even
now, the copper is where-
withal to other auricles, other

hearts. I stow them in Tesco
carrier bags, where the soil clings
on from yesterday's

potatoes. At ten pence,
five pence even, third-hand
or fourth, they're dirt-cheap for all

their showy binding. Old gold,
mock gold
lettering is vanity,
vanity. Our golden hours,
our golden treasury's

doubt distilled
and pent in hard covers
for all the world, dreaming on
this world... The cliché of
a withered flower still keeps

a place, between the leaves
in *Other Men's Flowers*. Now,
in the easy freedom of life and limb

I trudge on up the hill, hazily
haunted by some sense of

one broken-backed carrier
tense before collapse, not
able to see me home? Not

returning to the soil,
plastic bags will be
there, in the next millennium
waiting on us, if

we're... I swing up the other

bag, shoulder my sack of learning
and *fin de siècle* titles, innocent
as the world-weary... St Christopher
with the Christ child piggy-back. Without
a doubt, one or other

blurring text will open
my eyes. Certain writers are the living

dead: they still hawk
their losses and gold

daze around the hypothetical

future, their purple passages
for ever amber, ever
green. Grey, ghostly
confessors, they are our friends, unable

to betray "...I will go with thee." "And this
gives life to thee", even
as the yellow leaf falls a-

way, returning to the soil. So
in passing, books penetrate
in blinding perception:

their weak spines, sugary
past their must, their must

the thumbed turn-
down... marking
somebody's place, loss
of the power of concentration. The point is
retrievable under another

system of crossed life
lines? Straight as a die

or colonizing Roman road
in England, the road runs on
up hill. I'm going home,
still... I'd take my pilgrimage
with an armful of learning
for two pounds, fancy free.
Take it away now, scholar gypsies all!
Take it away, down Romany way!
"Everyman, I will go with thee,
and be thy guide, in thy most need
to go by thy side." *Rural Rides?*
Wild Wales? Shaw? *The Ring*

and the Book... you can't live without? Alexandra
...Mansel... Walter... Sketty... one name gives

ground to another, succeeding
each other in the sections of the dead

straight road, leading from Swansea
centre, post-war concrete. From nowhere

I remember that story of Cobbett
seeing a paper mill... once upon a time

a flour mill: "They seem to think
the people can eat books." Now,
it isn't Wales – or England –
but anywhere out of this world, first
world. Above this culture's come-on

in the bookshop window, a print
of Augustus John's portrait of
Dylan rides
high, drunkenly. He holds
sway over Everyman

classics, yesterday's tear-jerkers, clapped
out romance. Yesterday's
bodice-rippers, their jackets
tatty, impregnated with *Yellow
Book* muskiness, Penguins for ever amber

and all of the jumbled factions
with their *belles lettres* lie
...as they fell

from the dead hand

of fashion, changing
hands to the bookseller. Even
within a scholar's studied
shade, there are too many books ever

to read as... yet, couched in the way
of yesterday's sentence
and stops, signing the way

down all our ways. Else-
where, they look for bread

...for love or gilding faith
or cash or bread. Else-

where we read it up, gain in-
sight into their unbearable
confessional or Psyche. Here
are the old eternal

"windows to men's souls", where
we weep. The light of
day's slow infection
has burnt some books

like a dirty page of
history, pornography.

With a dotty discolouring

rash, they're pitted in
the light. Over

the hills and far away...
but with a scholar's hump
(making the worm turn?) ah
but the open country, fancy
free of the stacks, gone west
the pilgrim's pack, for ever at my back
their voices and the traffic near for
the kill. The siren voices of the living
dead... join with the evening
blackbird. Leaving the town
centre, I head for
the leafy – campus – west, branchy
between roofs, glimpses of
Swansea Bay between trees. I walk
into the golden sunset, going
home fast, with
my gilt killing.

Cleaner

I clean their rim of dirt,
my horizon's bound. For all
the world, this is how
it would have been

centuries hence,
knowing only my place
whence all my forebears came,

borne out of the same light of day.
Theirs is the day:
the view from their picture windows,
the scenic view, even the frosted

– semi-frosted – bathroom pane's. The rich have it
made. I wipe away for ever

until the raspberry of their porcelain
purely blushes, again. Their
wide washbasin's scooped
from *Harpers & Queen*, a glossy
"scallop shell
of quiet" affluence
to send them on their way
lavendered and fresh,
sprayed and deodorized. Washed
and scrubbed,

I make it good among
their private squalor,
left for the likes of me
knowing our place
is in their place,
cleaning up after them. I kneel to
the floor, stamped by
their soles, rubbing till I can see

shades of a shade of
the face they've ground
down centuries, mouthing:
I make it good among

clotted cream toothpaste
on their clogged toothbrushes,
stray body hair, and rose
of their scented talcum
on the rug. On hands and knees,
I wipe up after them,
like any mum after kids or

how a paternalistic society works. The lady of
the house projects her self
image in showy model dresses, *soigné*
suits. Among her rejects,

I paddle ankle-deep
through the silky pile, carpeting
her bedroom, wall to wall. (Who needs
to outdress the Oxfam shop?) I shake
yesterday's two killing outfits

and hang them.
I wipe away their spots and spills
and iron them out,

magicking away their
waste. I see Diana off…
out, with her eye-catching lines
and curves, but I am Di
and this is where I am:

I wipe in the wake of Joanna's
bubble bath and day

dream, *therefore I am*
Joan, and this is what I'm at:
dashing away with the Brillo pad
till you could see your toady mug –
oh greasy Joan! What of a self image?
And as I rub away, I see it all:

my dad was a milkman, I was
teethed on the National Health
and a beneficent state

taught me the 3 Rs plus
a thing or two, failing most of us
at eleven plus. But I've read
half the public library, fiddle
with poetry, and work
for Labour all along the line,
glad to have escaped being
centuries back

a peasant, labouring
for the likes of them,
among their chattels – serf,
albeit in a setting beautiful
in summer, even to work-grey eyes,
beyond this world's

dreaming on… Through
double-glazed panes, Brother Sun
beams on motes of dust, polluting
her carpet's virgin snow. God
– what of the sunny uplands, all our
ancient meadows? *Their* economic

necessity always wins out. As if your feet
were lead, you carry on. What
of the wrong

choices – no option –
washing me up (in a job, *yes*)
on this surf line, a dog's
body, doing for Mrs Whyte and her scum

up at the big house? With all
the county tone, through the mid 70s
it still survives... the taint of
the grosser functions
not quite "gone away,

gone far away into the silent land"
of out-of-date prescriptions and old

wives' regimens, despite rows of deodorants,
indestructible aerosprays, plastic
rank on rank. They've always aspired to keep
their shitty brass to keep

the scum away. I know
my own grey cells might
better theirs – as if brain
power matters. Why do I let them
...corrupt me, to doubt
a more equal way?

Pie in the Sky

Ours, in another world of certainties...
Their "script of joy", seeing them through this soil
that yields paper where it's written how
grass withereth, could yet have been our food
for thought, our staff of life to lean on? So
the bible would have still survived, well-thumbed,
intact. A one-time source of daily bread,

it serves here for a book end, propping light
verse, thrillers, "treasures upon earth, where moth
and rust doth corrupt". And silver-fish prey
on hosts of wafery words of God... changed
into lithe bristle-tails, and silver-scaled
like Victorian mock illumined script.
So thirty silver pieces, many times
over, flash, fade away on hallowed ground.
Transcended, through feeding the multitude
taking and eating as programmed by genes,
the word's made flesh and dwells among us, hosts
of skittering, flittering silver-fish.
Through starchy texts, these insects seize the day,
gutting our promise of pie in the sky.

A.I. in Paris

My little touch of worldly throw-away:
"Eric? I last saw him in Paris." "*Sous
les ponts...*" strolling seigneurial through wind-
fall golden hours, in amber... memory:

Le Monde in hand, he'd breezed, "Just blew in, hot
foot from L.A. for some symposium
about mentation." "Come again." The quay's
Sunset Boulevard... "Thoughts!" "I'm reading at
the Bibliothèque": yellow leaves and all
that fall... "Am I out of my element?"
he ejaculated (into A.I.
via seminars on Freud: "God, *time's* shit,
like gold" he'd proselytized in Penge). "Pr'aps
artificial intelligence isn't *me*?
This damned computer model's teaching us

it takes more brain to put one foot before
its fellow than for most high-fly maths..." Hush
Puppies pussyfoot through the yellow plane

leaves' soil. "What do your colleagues think?" "They'll get
there first. They'll get tenure. The race is to
the brightest." "Meritocrats, after all."

Rosemary's Baby

Divorced from here by memories of then

...I lapse from half-recollected talk to
what she hammers home, keyed up... black and white
sentence's continuo. "Fostered by
films, old northern *jeunesse dorée*, we've lived
half a lifetime, making of us what we'd
be... with an expectation of life, north-
aged." "Rosemary's son is seven", borne to
her at four, after the endless five-year plan
to adopt... a single person. After Wayne... new
image on my mind's video: Émile
with his new English, saying "Rose-marie
you are the friend of *all the world*." With her
son conquering a new world of mud, Rose-
mary at Greenham, fluent as may be...
fluted: "There's never any right to have
a child – not on your life. In this age of
bloody population explosion, in
a short-fuse world of widening dust bowls,
who on earth needs fertility drugs? Why
monthly bleeding's a northern luxury."

Sub-standard

Sack of potatoes dumped across a chair,
a crumpled skirt to wrap her body in
...she sags across the lintel of her life,
eyes on the talk, the rest of us at it.
Her beady eyes are bright for blessings, too.
Her arches dropped, her expectations lapse
into the shell of all the selves let slip,

dumb, dowdy, hanging on for dear life, still.
Clear morning died on her... the evening shades
allure the failure, evolution's miss.
Pity the ugly, cooped up in their rooms
in all the passion of the ill-favoured... rank:
today's birthmark, tomorrow's stigmata,
like some staccato stutter that isn't yet

a slur we find attractive, that fine nerved.
She's that fine nerved, paralysed being... teased
by loud-mouth friends to "make more" of herself.
Skimping for rent, she writes a "standard life"
yet can't deflect their comments, like their fags
stubbed out on her marble, too too solid flesh,
so puts on cotton gloves to take on life,

nursing her raw hands, nails gnawed to the quick.
Up some invisible ladder, man's eye crawls,
up one pale leg whose unveiling in June's
all of a piece with rats' tails of mouse hair,
a rudely smeared moustache, a heaviness
and all the clichés of the also-ran.
Mourning becomes that unloved youth, fills in

spaces between her table and bed. She's stripped
to wan lacunae by a gentle word,
that glancing... seesaws still her maelstrom mind,
thrown by any chance... fool mooning around

her room, snowed under by papers, dust drifts.
Fecundative spring tides flood her each month,
leaving her high and dry and feeling low

yet live. Light highlights where the carpet's frayed
tracks in between her table and bed, soft chair.
She falters midway, notes another thought
for all the world, a child arrested, still
frozen after the game: *les jeux sont faits*.
Iron will keep her marching on ice, like
death and the iron maiden – or old "old maid"!

Dead from the neck down's what she used to fear
they say. Who cares? Her life has uses, though
floored by disabling need for love. Poor fool,
poor curves, live... mind, and should some shaggy youth
con her, among the rest, "You're beautiful" –
skeleton key to day, that never came –
then would I want to slap his face or cringe?

Rejection, the Literary Life

But she hangs on, the sucker that she is
re. her own life. Sadly, unlike their Lives,
biographers don't need reasons to fail.
Once hers, too, could have been a standard life?
She's kept faith with her ghostly clientele,
casting their endless possibilities.
Doubting's a cast of thought, still more... self doubt:

"Jim wrote me, 'I might as well be from Mars,
nobody wants my work'." "Unlucky Jim,
still true to type." "'The literary life's
the potato count, food for tomorrow?
for how long...?' Food for thought, at least", you muse,

ploughing the furrow to the throw-away
end. First, third persons whirled down side by side

...everything's sublimated to what end?
All chance? Or was she floored before she quit
mum – sh – did she, in turn, get her fair share
of baby love? Podgy legs beat up, down
between table and bed, will peg out, so
...a track across their tracts, ankle-deep in
her sea of papers, rubbished in the end.

A Version of Tristan

La Pléiade edition – the book's washed up
with sere Left Bank *bouquins*. I net your soul
whose first edition was remaindered in
a brief, star-crossed life. Dear heart, *Les Amours*
jaunes... they had you in tow, your "actress" love
and her lover count. You'd barged in. You hugged
the shoulder of the coast, steering their light
pleasure craft. Your bed was a beached boat. Blocked
from your other love, wide sea, the sea! half
crippled from sixteen by arthritis, self

imaged as the also-ran... pariah... self
named for pain... painting with your penis in
ink... impressions of desolation row:
Bohemian Paris. An Eliot
"influence", Berryman's dedicatee
in *Love & Fame*, you'd have loved fame for you're

burning contempt and spurning, with the match
stick beats you whittled to crush beneath your sole:
Roscoff's salt breath blown out in Paris slums.
Ah si j'étais un peu compris! Yearned for,
for you... sails in the bay were always black
ink over paper, Tristan. Ah Trist, *triste*.

Black and White

"Some sheep are psychologically goats."
"Hell, we've all got damned individual
hang-ups. So have the goats. But they're ill-starred
and cheated by their birth. Our luxury's
to be emotional underdogs, half
identifying with pain you didn't have

to have. Grammar school kids like me had it
made." I file one nail with another, nod
greyly. "Living this quiet life, I've found
such vivid, mixed-up memories wash past,
colour the day." "I avoid memory",
cheating self images' old torture, still
savage caricature lying... in wait,

clouding the mirrors, people's eyes. She stares
out at the leaden estuary, sky
grey, as if her boat came in... memory's
repainted ship upon a painted Tay.
Marooned, I identify from her old

time-retouched London time, a clock, a mug,
an oldfashioned parchment lampshade not made
with human skin, washed up, in memory.

Onions and Tulips

Obscenely bulging... one leg of a pair
of laddered tights swings by the window: grey
brindle... more like pickling ones, doubtless home
grown, these sad onions look like tulip bulbs.
The starving Dutch ate *those* in the last world
war. "What do we do with our time?" "Write on

Meredith, myself, work with CND
– a bit." Rushing back to London, I stole
this green gift of the day. She speaks all in
...the dark, not seeing why on earth I ask
myself, reading my stare: "They're the most mild
tempered vegetable. I left some in
a black plastic sack, months. And they survived.
Sprouted" through their own wrenched tears. "Living on
spuds, never a meal they don't lift." Without
even the tang, it's the old madeleine cake
syndrome: I'm back in London, she still lives
there with slap-dash but never throw-away
style: lunch for friends – at four – raw onions and
rice. "We eat too much, here." Once Maud left... Ann
mocked lips lipsticked pink tulip, one skin stripped.

The Rotted House

1. *Ground of Our Being*

She's cleaning down the staircase, where she kneels
each day. A slammed door's gun-shot would topple her
head over heels down five plush floors to die.
Her overall flaps – game bird on its perch,
just? Rubbing along in rich people's steps,
she works out her bad temper on the wood.
Bulging arms wobble like apple jelly – beige.
Her face is raspberry. She's seeing red.
The wood drinks in her wax. Rushed to her head,
blood drowns out thought. *My arms are killing me.*
On gnarled knees, like a Christian climbing high,
she notices the sky-light needs a wipe,
rain-dark. Fearing even step-ladder heights,
she always hugs the floor, keeping her ground
though grounded on their magic carpet, frayed
with fretting for her high-rise flat that sways.

2. *Twilight Zone*

No more... do meter men like it down here,
however they smarm "Ma'am" at the old cows, ash
blondes. Any official intrudes down here.
With coinbox meters finely tuned or raped,
all that energy's burning itself out

on street corners and never lighting up
this twilight zone, rack-rented Rachmanesque.
They get us down, the ubiquitous file

shut up with tight lips, common entries. So
men from the ministry put in their oar,
foot in the door, keeping the road ajar.
They dog-nose into – and up – everything.
Their sights on cupboards, skeleton keys spoil
to show off... how barely Mother Hubbard is.
Meantime, *they* cry round compounds of the night
...the dogs of dogs, our one world's pariahs.

3. *Scene of the Crime*

Night... insects eavesdropping, the ceiling seeps
along the cornice, flowery with such fine

plaster dust, where the slates have flit. Downstairs,
the front door's fretting round a giving lock
– a breath of wind blows it in, but people like

us can't fear theft? What hopes! The likes of us
can't lose! Outside, another bent tramp drops

by. In the empty basement, things go bump –
some beast moved in. Lord Lucan? Derelict,

the house is stronger than all those high hopes
bringing in tenants, frayed at the edges now.
Petty crimes it's seen rankle in key holes, take

the gilt off evening sun, whose landlord's
taxes and heart attacks will shut him up.
I watch the house steal what belonged to us:
impalpably, a fine new wall rears up.

4. *The Rotted House*

Fall of the house of an habitué
of dim bedsitterland. Blonde fluff festoons
the dumb waiter beside Ms Havisham.
The bell-pull is redundant – couldn't hang
a flea. The dust is riddled here and crawls.

The stains crowding the walls up crooked stairs
are humped ghosts, knowing as... they couldn't be
alive. Milky newspapers in the hall
leak past disaster... cultivating fresh
crises, embodied in rotund earwigs.

So creepy-crawlies live their twilit day
in all the interstices of decay.
The house that Jack built... all fall down. It steals
pigeons' turtle-dove wing-beats, hurtling slates.
Will anything ever go well, here? May...
April again light through the fall's dead end?

5. *Missing the Bus?*

Her everlasting flowers swamp the glass.
Her fingers grip an occasional table,
ringless. She drums as if she waits to touch

a qwerty keyboard to pseudo-life. Sub-
librarian, she has no books round her

cluttered home. "Whatever jumble you can
spare..." My yearly begging call. Why do I
...suspect behind even these bull-frog eyes
old teenage dream, a princess dozing on

snow-bound, though crowned with thorns of briar? Divorced
from even her king of glory. First light,

she breasts the day down Victoria Street.
Neat on the kerb, in the shoes of the north,
she waits for the bus. There's no master plot
but our great expectations... the same road
will open without fail. With each new March.

6. *Summer of 72*

June breezes through sash windows, raised... from depths
she isn't even trying to relate
to their concern's "current... unemployed black
school leavers in Lambeth..." His grace notes draw
the month, which is as ever half an hour
out on the balcony, the tin-sheet floor
untouchable, bare-foot. Waspish, it stings
wan toes: everything's molten southward to
the Thames, non-stop behind the houses in
between... She'd glimpsed a pair of hippies, flopped
down in the dust, wherever they could be

themselves, one *patrie* under their soles. Could
anyone accept her if they knew her

trivial neuroses, house flies' buzz? Ann
with youth's flush and her *dirndl*'s cool, so at ease
with all... the world and Eric is the sting.

7. *Fustian*

Flaring, talk outlasted last drinks, last train

of thought. The last point hit home... "Ann, at least"
would live by her rhetoric's verve? Eve'd spun

a line about somebody's marriage to
some guy Jim had tarred "chauvinist pig": "So
dance into sacrament, computer date,
gathering peascods through *danse macabre*" – charmed
by the image's glad rags – "commodious masque,
heading a partner off. With words'cloth of
gold... Lothario hustles in the distaff side,
touching his own... 'to wive it wealthily'.
Why did he seek to tame the shrew, beshrew!
Though love a nag, her cunt's melliferous
as his untainted and mewling heir's name:
his son, honey, he ditto contracts for.
Gold ring lies... fairer through a porker's snout."

8. *Jim's Legacy*

More *savant* of self than philosophy
postgrad, flaxen hair bleached by the ancient pain,
the cruel sun dazzling his eyes vouchsafes
slight insight into muddy motives: "Yet
there'll never be any escape from that

seaside resort retired to by the old
stockbroker belt. Two warped Penelopes,
they would still weave fate, daily..." Parcae spin
their spidery thread like gut and cat's-cradle
the indifferent heir, fixed on the sun
...child difficultly born, blue in the face

with explication to ears deaf, now. You
will not see the sun go down on the lack-

lustre man they made from all our yesterdays
"with that umbilical cord of their tail
lashing whomever they'd conceived not... me."

9. *Nature, Nurture*

At first it hurt, festered... imagining
their kids playing over their floral lawn,
games overlooked by the everlasting elms
and cushioned by the weeds rampant on clay,
unless they'd banished them. And then, the trees
dying... his emerald isle retreat gone
down with Dutch elm disease, leaving the place
any Streatham house, softened that blow. Young

wild-haired mothers had made themselves at home
in their place, with love children, problem ones.
"We've all got our problems": wandering back...
thoughts flew into branches, that canopied
childhood's old never-never... blues. "In the end
we've earned our Labour Party membership",
he'd smiled in their bijou Highgate flat. Maud:
"It seems the squatters are our budding fate."

10. *On the Balcony, Next Door*

Look through the branches, mussed like jade pondweed,
down through the cramped tree's submarine green days...
down to the mossy flags, the lower plants,
where three urns bulge through green wine-bottle light.

This Pimlico backyard, mere, lush square feet,
riots between the tall house and walls... in
a green shade. Through fey dereliction pouts

bow-lipped, a most official climbing rose.
Creepers write time over... the whitewashed walls,
inside the secret garden, fusing all
but in light's swoon, gnats' element. They've traced
the crazy paving's chancey fissuring.

Their visitors would tilt a sunset glass,
mouthing sweet nothings at the happy hour:

"Delightful pocket handkerchief", on cue.
His divorce went through, while the wild touch grew.

11. *Talking to Yourself?*

A November poppy bleeds at my breast.
The stains crowding the wall up crooked stairs
are humped ghosts, pack-laden... Sternly, I climb
to that stone-eyed woman's room. She'll go on

explaining "...for the life of me, drained by
the last shock, naked, live power to lie
through his teeth." Truth? How to get through? How to
breathe life into the down-beat, dead-pan flow
and throw the mind... across the room a line?
Net curtains blanket an abandoned cycle

through that lapsing garden. Last... red rose. Long

weathered, a bird-bath rears, unfrozen yet,
the pedestal's an angel weeping "...yet
everything's relative." We're all like

gnomes paralysed in clover, here. *I*'d weep:
the countries and the airways in between...

12. *Moorgate, Passing on*

Imagination screams it's frightfully
smoothly the train slows... gone into the light:
fresh tiles, the smart adverts flash windows on
the world... a long dark tunnel and without
an ending, ending with the old... childhood things
down rabbit warrens of subconsciousness.

Last of the day's commuters sprawl across
stale compartments, exhaustion insulates.
Impassively, we've reined in the old nightmare,

ride out high hopes, behind glass frontages,
slot in and out, propping the system with
well-appointed lives that go like clockwork

through escalating tension, an eye on
The Times... riding our worries on to Bank.
The rat race is as ever, like the day
another crash is the end of all our lines.

13. *Correspondence*

"The letters say it all." They don't, you know,
yet gentle reader, she who runs may read
looping the loops... some plane dipping through grey
elision into the indecipherable.

The sense *is* smudged, I know... that's how it is,
spelling it out, our shop-soiled souls slope off.
The typescript slants from thesis into *texte*.
Sensitive pens stutter, flag stylishly,
shivering round the uniform white square.
"Today, what could survive of us will not

be airmail scrawl. Biros mean we'll remain
mortal." The words lie there; a sense subsumes

the signs, egging even serifs to dance.
The sun has set... a shade of meaning to
our hasty characters: dying at last,
a chance page fixed in amber... flies present.

14. *Gossiping over Lady Diana Cooper's Memoirs*

Ploughing is a very great new pleasure...
Letters embraced his Virgilian and Home
Guard life in that land of evacuees,
gas-masked into the rustling, rural dark.

Just post-war baby, Ann damns the book, reads
...an old self, weeping over "...of all things,
Diana Cooper's memoirs!" mock shocked. "All
human life is there." "Privilege's dead

wood." Sixteen weekly visits to help her
year's farming... war-work, *the happiest days
of my life*. And his farm near Frome, the beasts'
cycle. Duties. Toward the end, *like carrying*

a basket of stones to her in Algiers. *If
I had a wish... to carry your milk-pail...
If it were raining... do the crossword by
the fire.* Weakened, he died... digging for England.

15. *Snap-shots*

What power they still hold to move you, still
...life in the eyes, and jaundiced at the air:
blown generation. And when reproduced
by magazines, the mousy hair is fired
by sunlight to some flaxen-haired desired.
Their oldfashioned life-styles blanket you from
the real... electric shock of any art.
Their yellow photos: teas and camps, "Great" War

and love, among the haystacks... Bloomsberries,
sheep... images, they overlap, fixate
...simulacra in amber. Skidding on
..."the good minute"'s. You wish you hadn't looked
but I never saw what the butler did
but when a mind has haunted you the years...
time out of mind, the thought's off beam and fears...
the incredible actuality.

16. *"Let This Cup Pass from Me"*

Washing-up always gets done. After all
...*l'entre deux guerres* stripped ceremony, you pile
it on dish-washers, just the same: her new

lipstick stuck on a cup, cherry-streaked cream.
Their bloody bone china. Old servants' kids
no longer privy to rich nakedness,
not "little pitchers" who saw nothing, saw
all, understand according to our lights:
chance sorted this world's haves, have-nots within
the womb. That voided oneself on the stairs

scrubbed or climbed socially, according to
your lucky stars. The function of the rich
was to employ the likes of us, the great

mass of the people, lower orders, scum.
And so they gave some... work, and it was good
as God was saying via his clergymen.

17. *Dust*

In some of her homes, dust's the merest smear,
a feint for fingers flared to write names in
water on escritoire, piano. High-
lights in their gloss reflect where many hands
made light work? Or the square's pollen fused with
inner city rot has accreted, spared

bolts from the blue fallen out of clear skies.
Like now? The char dusts off planes and veneers
...sunlight dusting them up, golden again?
Rarely, rarely fallen to her lot, mink

crenellations of fluff and furry ash
camouflaging the rotted house. Sick time's

tongue has licked round the room and all... is like
a child's snow-globe, wherein we're all shook up

with deep dust and no new broom sweeping in.
A-tishoo! A-tishoo! We all fall down.

Circumscribed

"Hot air, Ann...", through the iced glass, her window on
the world, her Japanese transistor picks
up tinny sheen. The tuning band's a vein
red as traffic lights, off. "We'd breathe dissent
to the end, in this collusive iron grip
of sunset capitalism..." "And sunrise
hi-tech's scope?" "We were born sceptics, ripe for
a Russian hospital jail – else beneath
the notice of Big Brother, God! A shame

to be saved by your own failure – although
you've done some good work." But it's I, I, know,
who'd likely miss the flak. She knows, I know,
stonewalling for the weaker sister's sake
"...whitewashing propaganda, our half truth
we're circumscribed by?" "If half we hear's half
true..." in whose skull, neural hemisphere? "Say
– we'd leave reneging till the syringe pricked
our liberal bubble, dead keen to leave
a green globe spinning on, in doubt. Trust not
polluted to the flaming core by then,
and all of the green dreams blown in hot air."

Derelict Landlord

1. *Derelict Landlord*

Living and loving doesn't make it yours.
Flagged steps have come to sag beneath my step.
I've scrubbed around the landlord's hammer toe,
whose heavy tread surfaces through poor sleep.
These sticks of furniture, time and we've handled,
they'll send for scrap when he has got you out:
when I have gone away, gone far away

the landlord'll still be rolling in the dough.
The keys are in his hand, he mans the gate
up at his father's house: he sweeps the board.
The old man dropped dead, so rents rise sky-high.
The chips were down with Engels and Jack Straw.
All tenants to the barricades! The plea:
an Englishman's home's her castle or one room.

Sky, air is free for all. As for the birds…
your sleeping head, my love's – given notice.
And when you hit the sack for good, you're still
good for arrears. Beetle mania grabs
her, bangs her feather head between the walls.
She's down and floored. The Beatles tell her that
Penny Lane's not yours but courtesy of

the landlord in his roomy limousine,
hugging himself *all that* way to the bank,
the next street down: "In my father's house were
many rooms." Expanding, he crushes dolls'
houses under his feet. He's Jack the rip-
off peeping in back windows, sniffing each
storey's privation, snuffing privacy.

Stains up the stairs keep time with him. Well-fleshed,
well-heeled, he's easing up the long haul to
the windiest floor – the sky's the limit: his

breath would cloud our sky-light. God – his mailed fist
pounds, he puts in the boot, the salesman's soft
shoe in the door, shuffling her life ajar.
The house takes in all, with their rising scent

and hackles: "So who do you think owns the place?
I am a man of substance, wouldn't you know."
He has the cash, the manner and the nerve
or our wildfire grey cells *will* add up to
a live health risk brought home to him. In the end
the council'll clap an order on our – his
drain's flux. "So who do you think owns the street?"

The law is on your side. You need it, mate.
You aren't the insect underneath his sole.
You haven't got cash, only butterflies.
You haven't got a home and he owns rows.
Who said the nineteenth century is dead?
Let them eat cake – die – lust after rentbooks.
The well-fleshed landlord's sitting on our lives.

2. *Restoration*

Afternoon sun obliterates the pane.
Memory hangs fire, yellow in the light,
blurring the universal dust, blonde fuzz.
Next day, a strong-arm hammer bounces fluff
drubbing toward *de luxe* flats' high-rise rents.
Everything filters sticky plaster dust,
half of the house a rib-cage for what's left.

So, this ageing house is suffered to go
under the hammer, punishing its structure.
The insects and the secrets all come clean.
The shadows will not fall this way again.
And unexceptional masonry tilts
the corner that held Victorian them
never remarked by us, immersed in like

problems. Happy, perhaps, you wouldn't care
so much about the passing of the light
from that blocked frame. In one room at the top,
a sitting tenant fears the naked joists.
She fears the house left unfamiliar, stripped
of its old air – the accreted century's
taking in inmates with their rising scent.

Her hands will never be quite clean again.
The very walls that bounded her fall down.
Affronted, all her narrow being shrieks
softly from the housetops at new space,
old dreams, new boobies in the boarded night.
A trailing finger dips in history,
writing in dust, to varnish how it was.

...It was that dirty basement bathroom, shared
by all us tenants, earwigs and the dawn
sunlight flooding across the tiles, their white
grouted in nameless dark. It was the light
gold through the landing's long window, the air
alive with gilded dust's old high... For all
the house survived the blitz, he's guillotined

the light: the old days' rhythm... falls with that frame.
"I just called in to fill you in", he says
"to put you in the picture, as it were,
about the work in hand." The landlord waves
a lily-white palm, monarch of all that
surveyors see ripe for Improvement Grants.
"All this refurbishing – you know I've spent

a bomb on this. I've shelled out for your good
fortune..." No. You don't know, it's costing me
the earth... to see it go, the home I loved
for all of seven thin wan years, with all
the fantasy of younger hope, the hope
of moving on, sharing the light that frames.

The Picture in the Picture

Ducking highlights, back of her ram-rod back,
over her head, the picture's subject slides
out of the painted frame into the same
collusive dark, framed by the painting... "I

say, is the picture in the picture still

life?" *That* canvas, perhaps, slides from the frame
that eye'd have overlooked, reared on what frame?
First five years' flotsam? What's a painter but
a mandolin, piquantly echoing
shades of a shade of how it could still... be?
"You've killed the conversation dead." I see
poor Eric, still – "Is it all right to buy
a picture as investment, if you cry
over it too?" Ann shot him down. "People die
for art. The truth." "Truth's multiple, that's how
I read Cubism." "Bloody multiple truth." How

else tie time's fourth dimension down on to

the paper but sequentially? All art's
aleatory, for but for the grace
of chance conception, there's no eye to point
how light's picked out, scaling a ram-rod back.

In the Picture

Dust dyes... shades colour reproduction fires
from oils, fixed by the painter's inner eye.
I eyed this pin-up in her old flat, years
back. Not Picasso, must be Braque? A key

signature goes on beyond any bar
line. Air that the player plucks from the air's
picked out in swirls and echoed in the draped
design, the figure in the curtain folds,
with dying harmony, Fauve clash. Shade-tuned,
that deliquescing mandolin means that
player's black? Blossom and apple-green hint
about the figure in the autumn room
sends me back to her sitting there... flash-backed,
less boney under Twiggy's rule. She begged
flatly, "Why should the original be
worth any more?" "Ann, Ann, you could *see* it
for starters." *His* tone... flaring then, today

she talks with phrases hanging fire. Cut off,
half all the blackened clichés end "perhaps..."
finished off by thought? Sentences will join
up in silence, when all the colours fade.

In the Cage

Sky's uniform grey, black-braided by wires
like leading strings downhill into the mist,
that no-man's-land of cold war planes through rain

cloud skies. How to get through? How to breathe life
into the blackened clichés, throw the mind

across the room a line? Only connect,
looping the loop of hints... notes' lonesome trail,
till silence staunch the down-beat, dead-pan flow.
The automatic writing on my mind's
the shadow of adverts' sky-writing on
west blush-rose views. Wireless on, we've cried off
the real... imaginative leap, half hear
"You can't outlive your own... " colluding with

their cry: "Why do the voices come at me?"
All of the green dreams blowing in the wind,
setting the world on fire or our wildfire
grey cells... will add up to a thin red line
of me, drained by the last shock, naked, live
power to lie... across the tiles, their white
grouted in nameless dark... dying to say
"What price the global village, after all?"

Humanities' Computing Course (1979)

We hang around, waiting
on the outcome...

the print-out of in-
tractable exercises, in-
expert brain waves, the issue of

still-born brain children. Our grey
matter's exercised by fool-proof soft-

ware. With a turn-round of
a few minutes, only
connect... a computer

with another, far
away, in England. A Spaniard's
killing time, learning to play

the lute in Advisory: *homo
ludens... semper dolens*, shades
of Dowland. *Nolens volens*... it sounds like

some distant evening, played out

at some international workcamp, altogether
a far cry from
a review of the present state

of the art, careering to
the information society. Tying up
loose ends or purely number-
crunching, we're distractedly
doing our own thing, waiting
on the outcome...
on the last night, closing
open session, open forum. One
guy, Leo, fiddles

at a terminal
all evening, dead to

the world, scanning the screen
as the figures pass on

...across the humming lab, hanging
fire: a fair girl
in processed meat, some-
one from an anonymous Home

Office department, the pride
of academics going places with *Pet*
projects and inter-faculty interests
and students, learning Pascal, a new

language for programming – it's
the last night on the crash course! Some-
one leans on used print-out, gim-crack
house of cards, stacked against

the far wall, for the toddlers' play-group
to crayon over their way-
out signs and tottering

columns of figures...
stick men with
arms. One or other

of the gull
grey machines in the unit
judders into life,
jabbering print-out. One
or other of us makes

eye-contact, scanning "windows
into men's souls", and tears

off a strip
of wall-to-wall print-
out with a crack, cack-handed,
deviating from
the perforated edge. The man
in the dark suit shoots

his cuffs, frayed
in the lime light, the white

heat of technology, still
surviving. "Bright
eyes" or glazed,
the technicians are dead
beat. If we were less
of a motley and mad

bunch of live wires, dead
keen, everyone would be

on edge, and torn to
shreds. The lime strip
lighting picks out a frayed

hem on jeans' legs. Through
the open window, thoughts cycle
past, blowing in the wind
through the greenwood
as it were, around this lab
in bureaucratically re-
christened Dyfed. Time and

again, the print-out's torn
jagged, with its staggering
calculation, bearing it out
even to the edge

of the page. There's
the infinite

wallpaper joke, never
seeming to pall – after
all, it's the last night

for Pascal! And on cue, a mind
flashes up: "We are

using our own skins for wall-
paper and we cannot win." The image
is all, now *the medium is
the message*: the writing

on the wall, on the cathode
ray tube screen, with each light
pen. Once upon a time

Big Brother haunted the wood, now
pulped for the user-

friendly machine, made in
our image. Way out, white,

benighted crosses mark marked
trees. The medium's
all of the trees
that fall
in the sacred wood:

their shade's... flitting. At the end

of the day, there's half-
hearted talk about
"computer people", for the user-
friendly hardware, for the term

"humanware" wouldn't go down, in-
famously in the humanities. Where count-
less Middle Age angels danced
on a pinhead (and who then guarded
the guardians, theoretically?), a chip
receives finite live charges to the n-th power. How
else live, save

...as sceptical backwoodsmen, since we can't
even see the wood
for the trees, that fall

under a cloud, mushroom-dark?
Outside, in the dark,
over the hills and far
out, in mid-Wales and beyond...
drop-outs and some with means
ingenuously turn back to self
sufficiency, candidly digging
notre jardin. Through their dream,
a desert blooms, over the hills. And
far away... men marched to Catraeth,
defensive, to

their technological limit.
Historians of the future
will count more quickly, number-
crunching with abandon
the men who marched away,
who went without

historians, computing
like greased lightning
all of our vital statistics,
if we survive. So far, the race
has gone to the fittest,
watching for sheep and doom
over the hills and far away?

Dandelion

Time out of mind, the ground was frozen
iron. Then over night, there was a patch of garden,
a sea of yellow heads. Who'd have the heart
to hack these Goldylocks?

So now a thousand ethereal heads blow there.
So many short-fuse clocks are blowing in the wind. Yet

in the light, each one looks like
a crystal ball where you look to the future, remembering

it's only a matter of time
before like us they multiply themselves, many times

over. Grubbing them up now, I'd only scatter
the good seed on the land.
In his own good time, left

to his own devices, nature
will do his own thing. Through photosynthesis
dent-de-lion, the cat's-paw of the wild,
translated the good earth
into near meadow, now dying from the *communitaire*
land. There flowered a corner of
old meadow, swimmy with gold

early summer, buttercups
soon. Each cobwebbed head holds a candle to
each older child's cloud cuckoo land. But
one of their countless clocks moves
the heart like a pacemaker, limping home.

After the Programme

Once in a blue moon, somewhere or

other, I watch TV. Tonight will stick
in my mind, gilded in passing
in this gloomy barn
of a Television Room: saw-dust

and tinsel sound-track from the next
of many rooms, this dusty
floor in the Students' Union. It's mounted
more like a cinema screen or
Big Brother... with myself glued
to it, for the first time ever
mesmerized like a Zvengali's green dupe

in a film a friend was
working on, years
past. Students – almost an old
self image – drift past: in

and out, this room's a through-way
between others... in twos or
threes or going home, down
mean streets, *on the street*

where... huddled into a raincoat, he
reminded me like second sight
of X. At first sight, there was no ground

for so identifying, really
something in the way you
walked... these two years, two Is,
"bright eyes", staring

"windows into men's souls"? Giving
as I believed you

wanted, wanted I wanted... I
suppose I should give
secular thanks, if only for being able to

write a bit and go home
fast, under the stars... Still,

something about that
feature, in the man's habitual pose, recalled
me Y... *you only wasted*

my precious time as the Dylan song goes. Late
20s, early 30s was
another crucial

time? So in our generation, we number-
crunch, like the computer

simulations we are. For the rest,
everything has to be for-
given on account of the other

causes, effects: A, B, C. Why...
didn't I ask for everything

I got? And more? Still,
the mind's thrown by another

eternal triangle: on all fours, it
begs an alternative... society
being what it is. It's so

many genetical constructs, after
the programmes and chance. If
acceptance is only gushed

good moments, surf, starry
eyed in the dark
night of the soul... being

struck down into a wheelchair, you
mightn't venture even this far

toward "forgiving"? Always,
the given's

for accepting the wildly different
circumstances, similarly accruing
to form each one's

final zero. Sooner
or later. The programme included
toward the end, the two figures
arms round each other
walking across the green, green grass.

That green haunted me, wanting
love...

Drawing the Curtain

Drawing the curtain on the day,
the dun and mist, the white

...I turn in on my dusty room,
a litter of living and newspapers.

At dusk, it's hard not to be

yearning after skeletal trees, the Tay
unwound to sea with drowned
dreams... lengthening days. Away
from the front

of this block, you don't hear the thunder
of the traffic, back-firing
past on the road to Dundee,
past the city's Western Cemetery.

Greys and dun compose the day,
that would stick in my mind
and in the sinking light is
gilded in passing

like the odd purple patch
of heather,
and beyond the pale

flowers o' the forest
at the iron gate
at the necropolis, just
down the road.

Ann, Intimations

If nothing else, our fear unites us now,
whistled down even country telegraph wires
still spelling out in sere and khaki leaves
les amours jaunes of "Great" War wires, cut off.
Their writing on... battleship-grey sky's barbed
wire fencing off the day. So wires extend
our nerves to febrile antennae, erect

for ever in some fight or flight syndrome,
as Ann looks down at my "But don't you miss
the bright lights, ever?" "Not after all this
time." Maybe I hit home, though I didn't mean
to go so near the bone. So why must I
intuit things despite myself, and Ann
...never a close friend? Closer after Rose-

mary left London, her old confidante,
through friendship's mild, self-seeking *mariage
de convenance* until she moved on, too.
"Only connect", until you're pinioned by
a tangle of nerves. The sky's trip-wire's crossed with
the strings of puppets... of ourselves. And there's
never *une histoire à clef* but some key

work under *noms de plume*. Across the room,
the spaces in between... my twitchy nerves
join up with phrases and the tones, *that spring
...*to mind from her dashed letters' scrawl to form
a charcoal skeleton, a sketch of her
coloured by intuitions, blind insights,
memories... *mélange adultère de tout*:

that picture by her teases me, again.
Who else but Braque, for who else could have how
else tied time's fourth dimension down on to
the canvas but sequentially? A life-

time back she said, "I'm going outside now,
for vegetables for lunch", unmoving, out-
staring the storm sky, grey with life. And still

I read the figure in the carpet, like
divisions on a ground, the echo of
the automatic writing on my mind:
an Ann. Her mind's *vers libre* dying fall
counterpoints the other heart-beat drumming beat,
my dense narrating of a self beside
the eternal other, A.N. Other. So

was it different, hunched in some cave mouth
between sharp teeth of rock, deep throat of stone,
a red coal spat from amber licking flames?
Soon, with the blackened cliché of a grunt,
someone was scrunching charcoal over rock
worn smooth, puzzling over the opposing form,
playing with fire, pure Stone Age reportage.

In the Green-house

Uniform grey Fife sky's a window on
the world, framing a March, north-east view. "In
a nuclear family, you'd care...?" "We're all
in... the extended nuclear family." Stacked
leaflets shadow a glossy view of Cos

lettuce: the seed pack flares June, hybridized
beyond the likes of any medieval
dandelion-eater. Some've had stones changed for
bread, through green revolution... "And the Green
revolution, to leave our ruddy globe
revolving on?" "Four steps forward, three steps
back. Who looks to the green go-light to go

on for ever? And how can we work, save
out of the soil of slum committee rooms
through swirled fag smoke that gets in all our eyes,
fluffing the problems faster than we can

see through them, like carbon dioxide round
a deforested globe?" "Forty years on,
'the green-house effect'll leave the Soviets
the world's bread-basket? The climacteric
if..." "People in glass houses shouldn't throw things."

For ever Amber

To fill a gap, yawned in our idle talk
like waiting for the traffic lights to change,
I prise an orange Penguin from her shelves
– Holroyd's *Strachey*. I leaf through notes, their teas,
"Great" War and yellow photos, chancing on
a minute... luckless fly spreadeagled on
the margin of the text – out of line, fey
spatter of colon and full stops. It breathes
an August lawn: deck-chairs with Socialists
whose servants wait... By chance half-vacuumed by
a bare fore-arm's fan of follicled hair
– the gentle reader as God – it wasn't killed
for sport. A chapter's whited sepulchre
of mayfly motives' cobweb toils "shutts up
the storye" of the day. The minute flies...
fixed in the amber of the passage, still
dyed in the light, bloody old gold stains. Stopped

still in mid-flight, between green and red leaves,
fresh blood and green dreams, blowing in the wind
through amber daze, the long hot summer goes...
marching on, we inch to equality
for more of us, for sharing in the sun.

Thin Red Line

"Who wants a house-husband in her hair?" "Christ
– who wants a house-person?" Where servants lugged
coal scuttles for the lily-palmed, the fire's
one bar glows red rose at the hearth. "What's love

that made you... lie and bang your head against
the floor, time out of mind, days'... daze: to stop
thinking, hot for the certainty you're not

needed by the other? Why hang on... words' thread
into the bloody labyrinth?" Her hair's
auburn, a-quiver with barbed rhetoric,
red arrows: "...that moaned merging of the red
line of the figure in the carpet with
the figure in my mind's warp, straining to
see why?" "Like Sue." Lines of thought intersect
in mutual grimace at our memories
of green-eyed Susan, wearing her dear heart
high on her tear-rotted sleeve. And she so
old, in youth. "Anything that hit me here's
light relief since London. No one'll take me

so close suicide again. *I*'ll name that day.
Red letter day!" Well, she's lived. Sue? Me? Jim?

Woman with Green Eyes

That early morning mist that clings on through
the day, the year... high summer blinds her with:
before the grass is dying, green to dun,
she'll fall down on it. Dusty answers pall.
Rounding the square: why does she still believe
in love? Why don't you see it for mirage?
Only home traffic's blowing in the wind.

She knows that she should be resilient
to the air's lift across Green Park in June,
should venture praise, unbutton into smiles
at not so small mercies like life and limb.
In Oxfam photographs her guilt survives,
still... life of photogenic friends makes her
envy their families and futures, both

approximating ghastly glossy mags
and colour supplements? As for the rest,
they're... shades from books and half-cognizance of
their brief encounters crowds out autumn daze.
The vivid colours, they are there somewhere
...the lemon sun that warms even new year
before it's only photos dying, dun.

Stood up by her high pane, Saturday dawned
light on the window-box, the page, *The Times*
– *they are a-changing*, still... she lacks the nerve
for life. Her blood's greenery-yallery,
her mourning's shade. She watches with green eyes
the families of friends, the friends of friends,
their rosy affection and golden days!

Or earthy, her mood's gall acidifies
yellow October, ruddy shades that fall.
She focuses on life an evil eye,
mouthing alone as they emote on, loved.
Her look is jaundiced and her lip is thick,
her speech is dry, her tongue not dry enough.
The violet hour's... taxi! She's wanting out

green and yellow melancholy! Why not
go out into the highways and dive bars,
bringing one in, make, do and shift, shiftless,
till all the colours fade, dim eyes highlight
lyric momently lapsed past all belief?

And so before begun, his end is in
...the mist, seeped in the spaces in between.

A patch of green is always there, somewhere
even in London, bombed-out, swinging, high
– a blade of grass that seeing is to miss.
She withdraws at the slur of toddlers' talk.
Time-bombed, time takes in trust all that she might
have had and lost, tragedy of a split
second, *alter ego*... the car may miss.

Society incorporates the gay
– widows... the unfulfilled to weep alone.
Who knows the dark recesses of old homes?
Nuclear families' fissured cells are like
Bluebeard's. In the end, we're all alone, aren't you
both? Pity the ones who eat alone each night.
Save me the mauled divorcé! And again,

society makes her green eyes always smart.
When all's said and done, we're sad animals
who go in two by two and come out three
– oh child of our time! Partners freak out with
their mortgaged love and pretty... childlike things.
Pity the ugly cooped up by themselves,
who only stand and wait, eternally.

Framed by dull panes, they're squinting out, poor dears,
wasting their lives for ever looking on
everyone out there getting on with it.
They didn't have their children torn from them,
they didn't have their spouses lost or strayed,
kisses down phones, such childish crosses through
the mail. And tugging always they didn't have

love... wasting through their timid hanker, still
there are "green days in forests and blue days..."
Often and often in her... callow youth's

flashback, another... life trysts yellow love?
Now, she's a faithful work-horse, half a life-
time's work her own lovelorn identity,
still smiling through. Her colleagues call her kind.

Greengrocers' holly pricks her womb each year:
the crucifixion of Christmas, the time
for children? Faltering before her still
borne possibility, she's bleeding for
orphans and all objects of charity,
identifying with... nose on the pane.
Her life's a moving picture, looked down on:

a youngster's tenant, she stands by the pane.
She's not inadequate – oh no! – she's just
unlucky in life's draw, has drawn a blank
cheque on a dud self, against life, against
death and God, some of us die more alone!
Thanks be, the spring... romantic self's long passed
on, so she's glad to feel, tear-jerky, still.

Deep freeze: the flowers fade, the sparrows fall.
Oh where have all the good companions gone
– booked for for ever, boxed in tower blocks
with magic casements, insulating from
aural pollution and autumn in June?
Her pane is frosted with acceptance, forced
she'll plough her furrow to the bitter end.

Never Such Light

(1981)

1. *Never Such Light*

Never such light twilight. May...
April again light...! I read on, then
birds' chatter before 5 a.m., for

time's haywire. And so he could age
before my eyes, if there were time

to come to know the other more:
I've never more wanted to live

tomorrow, and tomorrow, and... Again,
with the radio news never blander, sometimes
it seems, after Reagan's land-
slide advent in the fall,
we all hang

together, on a pundit's lip:
"to the end of our

days", seeing the windy trees bud
after winter's hoar-frost,
iron past... May

...*rapport* exist, this day and age
after the late 30s, 50s?
A thought streaked white
like hair, like

                2. *In Love*

The lock's snapped and
the outer door's slammed and

tested... shaken
for the night. It's borne in on me,
this sun-rich May, going
home after the day's slog
at the office, late on this "long
and winding road", running
straight as a die

out to the rich gardens, their
shade and sylvan
imagos, out from the inner

city façades and wynds and
riverside sidings, universally
down at heel, with faces
infinitely drawn

into Dundee's dusty golden
sunset: with pitfalls and curbs
at every other
step, even love couldn't outlive
health. If the overwrought mind really slipped
from our wound-up

real...? And then, back of the mind,
the past prompts you, you know

in the place of the image now softening your –
mind, in that neural lumber-room,
you'll most likely be left

a gilded portrait, framed

with wormwood. Under wraps, for
ever... and again, with doting
delusion comes

the doubt, the doubt. Why

am I... the fall guy for that living doll?
Do women and men differ, at heart?
Will you still love me when I'm forty-four?
Will the real Dorian Gray
please stand up? *Snap-*

shot image: that con-

genital liar, whom
you took five years

to believe: everything's to be
forgiven for God's sake – "hold your tongue
and let me" –
love, and the usual

fear of the hurt dog look
in eyes. The divorced figures cry
that if you can't

settle for parallel ways, like
railway lines that only seem to meet

in the end, make it
alone, if you can. Who'd
take her life

in her hands to reach
a damp and burning hand, touching
a living image into life?
A man passes me by, down

at heel in blue suede shoes, walking
his golden cocker spaniel, his padding

soft with mongrel affection – and well

being. And in the end, even the self image isn't
lovable, doggedly ready for
nothing. Image it infinitely, ultimately good for

nothing... just... lost in multiple

personality. Some of us are repeating who,
who has love enough for all this – the sunless dead

time, and again "sans taste, sans everything" apart

from hurts of a younger you, a half-killed soul,
a half-life lifting in the sunlit daze?

3. *May We See*

Looking toward summer's
Lyonesse, I gaze at forget-me-nots
colonizing across the garden, next door.
The air's pungent, after all the bloody
rain, after drenching sun
light. A spider's thread catches

whenever our paths cross, across a room.
Blind to the others, I talk to his eyes:

so precarious a line
ten years ago, I'd have left in tears.
Or said my piece: *finding you enigmatic*
on your ground, where my sole
Scottish grandparent mayn't be enough

in your eyes? If they give any of us time...
Protesting, we're pulled in under the mushroom
cloud of our generation's phoney peace,
in the fat lands of the northern hemi-

sphere. If my eye can cry for love in ten years, I
may have learnt to cut it out

for another "philo-
sophy of life"... May
one ever come to

live with one
self, with the hereditary
nurture of self, nature of history's

"auld alliance" of hamlet and gene?
Only in England or France may I forget

being English, of course: "Ma Patrie...
elle est par le monde." Under a sky, white,

light blue, with branches in saltire,
in an aura of carbon monoxide, tourists drive past
on the road to Perth, the romantic Highlands
and the battle sites.

4. *Copper Beech*

As if by dint of the sight

...he came close
again, how often I look out to the hills
and mud flats of the Tay estuary,
and how mistily see beyond

leaves, with a bloom
like black grapes... midnight
blue's drowned in maroons.

There's always this tree against the green,
the grass and trees, lighting
my eyes... a shimmer of leaves, port
wine-stained, shuffled on

a breath. There's always
a breeze, shifting leaves.

5. *Dead Moths*

Their fall into the bin's

almost imperceptible,
deadened, tinny.

Taking out moths

from the dustpan, dimly
I wonder again if we'll draw
closer? So I hold a candle to the intention,
to whom might have been

...an old flame. Through the light
nights I read late, burning
the midnight oil, blood chilled

by the black and white
designs of characters, finally

dazed. I pick up moths in scores
in the space of a few days,
this summer of squalls
and trees combed by the wind,
leaving me glad
to huddle at the hearth
at twilight. Hoping to

avoid the fall
of a flutter-by

heart battered by the light-
shade of my reading lamp,
I distractedly switch on

and off. They're still

perfectly camouflaged on the neutral carpet
that goes with the room, matching
each passing tenant's fancy
free. In my partial vision,
in moths' grey and dun,
I see your eyes and hope

as midsummer blows toward
the fall... How many more

years shall we leave our-
selves? The radio news crackles
in the light of their conviction,
radiating all their
ends, and ours.

6. *Moonlight and Thistles*

It's another close clinging night in early spring.
It's the start of the suicide season, as the sad
figures bring home to us. Passing... a garden

down the road, I saw snowdrops,
ringed by grey guard leaves, pallid
pin-pricks of light, never such light.

Later, indoors, and highlighting the dust
and reflecting off the river, like foil,
moonlight streams through the wide window,

closed but wide open to night
...too bright for sleep and yet
too dark for dreams.

Sometimes this winter, moonlight
was light enough to read a book by
...casting shadows.

The phone has a tinny sheen. In this light,
any sentence rings false. Time and again,
I try to understand... so eerily

like treading water. Yet, I'll hit rock bottom:
he didn't care, after all. I'll catch the drift,
more in my depth in the shallows of shadowy reality,

daily. My eyes stray off, out, over
"the silvery Tay". From the window,
wide like a bay, water lies under moonshine.

       7. Pathetic Fallacy

Year round, I watch the wide river
unwound to sea, misty, white
...light through the dun landscape

and the honking
of wild geese was heart's ease
winter nights, first light.

It was a superfluity of self
seeping over the winter lands-
cape, with tears of light.

Here, there is the one view
and up-river he saw much the same,
I felt, drawn by the wide prospect.

My breath's mist on the pane and
nothing... outside the sunlight,
lighting people's eyes.

Other Men's Flowers

To fill a gap, yawned in our idle talk,
I pick a yellowing book from her shelves.
Dyed in the light, leaves open at a place
kept with a withered flower. Buttercup?
Plucked with a gracious bend, pressed by what fair
and fond, whiter than white Georgian hand
in some other life, seed that wasn't...? It was

aborted by the pressing, ravishing
white hand. The golden head lies... long cut off
dead head, ever cradled to some swan neck?
All their long hot summers were on the back
of servants, never asked to choose between
guns or butter. Grim, grey, she looks across
the gap: the war to end all... But chin up,

pale with her lilac sweatshirt, "I picked up
that Brooke years back, second-hand." "'Frieda from
Dan, Happy Birthday, 1915'." "You
fear that fly-leaf's..." "Heart-searching, we were spared
through battles where we didn't have to die."
"Time and sex saved us from surviving them...
tarred with white feathers, C.O.s behind bars."

Northern Ireland Peace March, London
25 November 1976

>"The grass withereth",
>trampled to mud
>as everyone mills round, ploughing up
>Speakers' Corner, "that is for ever
>
>England." Come together
>now, we churn this "richer dust",
>our soil. Look back, whenever war is
>
>switched
>
>on TV. Look in on history
>for our sins, the sins of
>the fathers visited on the unborn.
>Splashing the grass red, madder

leaves are dying in the fall, blood
red, yellow and gold, Vandyke
browns, that shade... in black

and tans, scarlet like a red-coat
or Flanders poppy, ploughed
back to mud. The trees bear

ragged banners, russet
and plum. Media-dubbed "ordinary
housewife", Betty Williams says
to the multitude "God sent

a fine day." The crowd's out
in force: ones and twos out
of suburbia, where two or three
are gathered together in
one of God's names... Anglo-

Catholics, ethnic minorities, Norwegians,
Quakers, lone wolves, Scouts, Jews,
Jewish Scouts, churches and minorities. One
parent and nuclear families.
Banners point to home

towns, whose out of the way
faiths overlap in common
cause with starry-eyed agnostics. They're

here from all the misty shires.
God-fearing citizens are up from their

God's little acres. And *La France* arrives, winning
a *blasé* cheer! Christians from all over
the green and pleasant land; Black
Country coachloads; closet
pantheists and fantasizing phobics
fighting secret battles to

the bitter end: a lively party
from that anachronism, St Marylebone
Grammar School: the salt of the earth
up from the garden of England,
down from the heart of England,
God's little acres, and beyond
little England's fringes: Glasgow,
Kirkcaldy, Cardiff, Celtica –
Cornwall? – called to the colours
of their marker flags: Northern
Ireland, blue and white after
blue for the internationals and
white for Wales, Scotland and Northern

England. As for the rest of
old England's map – brown, yellow and

harmlessly contained now,
pink... The dangerous colours are shunned
delicately – the green, the orange

and the red, flared at Marble Arch
by the battery of sun-dimmed traffic lights
our first contingent's squaring up toward. So
the war baby generation, breast
by breast with the next, white-faced
in red and blue anoraks, nuclear-age
veterans, *jeunesse dorée*, mixing it with the grey,
all of the shifting shades will march from these sods
and leg it toward St Martin's in the Fields.

Contingents hailing from the most far-flung
corners within these emerald isles
leave Hyde Park first. So
shall the first be last
and the last shall stand at the back
at the final rally in Trafalgar Square,
while a few brazenly cling on to

the monumentally comic lions
– but sure and don't tweak a lion's tail!
And the dead are lying

doggo, like time bombs. For us,
the inner city locals who came up the road
on Inner Circle home ground,
for once outside the rush
hour, there are hours
to stand and stare, size up
the individual in
the motley, between the head of
the march, leading off with Northern
Ireland and the internationals,

and the last London lot,
leaving behind the sovereign
turf half-ploughed. We go late
in the gauzy morning glory
of this royal park, thick fuzz
in the yawning space between the mist
and pleasant land. From Slough,
they took their pilgrimage, clutching at
sandwiches, hope's true gage. And all
around the Green Belt, home
county outfits made it into town
via Green Line: rag, tag and
blue jeans – the wearing of the green
mock army fatigues some camouflage
for humanity! And some of the everyday
nice kill-joys of the suburbs'
neat semi-s also sweep past,
all Queen Mum pastel

shades: moss-rose, apple-
green... hearts on sleeve,
even folksy. "And when I wore my apron
low" lilted that old Joan Baez lyric. "Green-

sleeves was my heart of
gold": gold ever lying
at the core, at the root of
all... at the heart of the matter.
At the Pentagon March, that green

field of the Cloth of Gold, as action-
painted by Mailer, "the dress ball was going
into battle": "We shall overcome..."
Now, sober suburbia, institutional
turn-outs, drop-outs and the eternal young
march to ask we don't know whom

"Give peace a chance", deathly hushed.
And so the Peace People vote with their feet
by Westminster Cathedral, risen now
high over Victoria Street's high rise

out of the waste land demolition drilled.
Under post-war offices and the Army

and Navy Stores, we'll process round to
the Abbey. So scenic, under an English heaven.
Under London's blue weekend sky,
Ireland's "a far-away country..."

In the mid 70s, the troubles
exploded in London, Caterham, Birmingham.
They brought them home to us. They also hit
an image of the green

and pleasant land. Up front, the stars
lead on... that "ordinary housewife" Betty Williams and
mid-thirties Baez, looking too staid
to "sail away", save

in humanity's ark. If only

each demo were its own end.
Onward, Free Church faithful, marching as to
peace, that promised land, with beads
and jingle-bells. Today, who'd dare to have a dream

this day lighting such a candle in England
as "shall never be put out" – an Olympic
flame for peace? Peace to
the hell-fire drivers killing time

and Hell's Angels. At Hyde Park Corner
with all the lights gone dim,
cheerful coppers (after all, this is
England) with gloves on – white – hold up
the traffic in glittering ranks,

lane after lane, beyond the green,
green grass and autumn trees,
as the people pass over

roughly ten abreast, as asked. Senior
citizens with push-chairs, manual
workers, white-collar, multi-colour

anoraked, we progress along Victoria Street
toward Dean's Yard and the mother of
Westminster-type democracies.
(Westminster doesn't understand far-flung
Cornwall.) Someone dishes out

leaflets to some marchers. Fighting
to get the Brit security

force out of Northern Ireland,
Troops Out attack the *Peace People*
for wanting peace at any price,
peace in our time
...in our lifetime. It's just

peace is the word to bring us,

sheepish, out on the streets.
And what can mere English do, save
spare one Saturday and hope against hope
a mainland IRA bomb never

has my name on it, odds on at a thousand to
one? The sins of the fathers are visited
on the children. We march

against the bombs or the bomb.

What moves more than a slow march
of the people, standing up to be counted
here and now, this day of grace,
protesting to the elected government
as of now, as of right? "(Boots – boots
– boots – boots – movin' up and...)" even if

the rhythm only aspires,
the people's flag is deepest red or
whatever the colour of
your lost cause, seen through

amber sun, with the green dreams blowing
in the wind, till all the colours fade
in darkened traffic lights, police-
controlled, and calloused feet
collusively softened along our way

of life. It's hardly
a *via dolorosa* for the likes
of us. Come out too, the gay
would be around somewhere. Behind ragged
banners, our souls

go marching on. And
did those feet in recent time
walk upon "the U.K.'s" pavement, grey Falls Road,
Andersonstown, over the water, on

the streets of London or "old Durham town",
Birmingham, Hull, St Helen's, even as
the shadow of a shade? We may not know,
we cannot tell the next man's killing strain.
A willowy youth, a handbag under arm,
falls into step beside two middle-aged.
October youth, greening toward
the fêted future, tread softly for you
have all the green years, flowering hopefully,

like all our kind hearts on sleeves:
each one a "bundle of contradictions"
and the light and shade of each,
wrapped in a unique care:
the man in the street, kind Mrs Smith,
the man on the Clapham omnibus
wanting the easy life like me, like
the next person, out on the street: all
the world's odd fellow or childlike,
with flare of youth or new found
land of the middle years. And awkwardly we pass on

breast by breast, but not speaking,
not I, not you, not the English,
not you, not I, half-choked and petty

bourgeois at heart. For many, the 60s are
heart's-ease of Baez' voice, against the gold
light of a youth of never having it

so good, never again, *jeunesse dorée*,
against the pavement-grey, the everyday
against the night: the pick-up picked up light,

the record repeated, that voice turned on
half of a generation, fine flower

power. A little lady from the home
counties wrote up a diary as she was
"here in Hyde Park", the light and shade of her
flying script of joy, pins from her top-knot.
"It was only a dream of a golden world",
the sun going down on our peace. Through sun
beams' dazzle dust, she sees some brazen girl
or else she thinks it from the looks of her

yet – pained – some fond thought, fair intent led to
a just putting the best foot forward so's
to do something and not to let grass grow
under us. Yet, over the dead, the green,
green grass of home grows long. After the rally,
history'll be seen through – that gold standard

held in a glass: some of us will look in
at the Old Shades pub, beyond the Cenotaph.
En route, the quick steps slur, till they fall out
of time. After the rally in Trafalgar Square,
after we've sung "Morning has broken, like
the first morning, blackbird has spoken..."
the camera-crews will switch the stars off, quick.
– After these monster marches, they call for
tomorrow's stage, bringing it all back
home, with more community work.
After the rally, leading lights dead-beat
off screen, starlings' early nightfall, the flock
departed... we'll go home to grass roots.

Going Home

1. *Across the Yard*

It is the moment of the lighting of
the lamps. They flare. As for the Lares' flare
...a groped switch's homecoming: "Lara's Theme" taped.
Dusk falls at six, the lighting of the year
stood off a while, while dark creeps up on us
whose bedsit homecomings are via Green Park.
Storm clouds are nothing, all over Europe now

the lamps are going... on. Evening, again.
Chancey illumination like the sun
picks out a rainbow chequering among
day's rows of warder eyes of tenements
keeping the day, our window on the world,
twilit: whose oranges and lemons, plonk
glowing against a donkey coat, dun dusk

darkened in orange and rose panes of light
against the night's black-out. I'm framed against
a long window, uncurtained, open sash
overlooking a builder's yard, once mews,
across the houses in between... Eyes get
across tomorrow with "the hopes and fears
of all the years" that met in yesterday.

2. *By Half-light*

Across the many whys, I weep which one's
the window on our cold... sea from your place?
I never noticed, look to sea... guess blind,
looking across the fields to your light,
looking between the elms' sway to the gale.
The block of flats blinks on home or away
across the playing fields, drawn to the sea.

A twilight zone, another... past life comes
to my mind's eye: the uncurtained, open sash
where I watched dusk come in in gilded yards.
Some old perception's standing as I see
a figure in a half-lit frame who's you
...I guess. And I believe summer may come,
net curtains blowing like perception's flux:

the human figure is a minute length
against the light, the dark, sea by the shore.
Climbing the hill from work, dusk dying fast,
I see the angle of perception shift
the lit gap in the curtains... narrowing
till everything gets lost in one more night,
passing on and by, by.

3. *Going Home*

Soon, winter will black out all afternoon.
Even at 3 o'clock, on sky's spring tide,
the day's a sick rose, flushed and dying fast;
heaven's a blush rose, reddened past belief.
Last of the gaudy summer daze... may still
transcend some of November's golden days,
early on in the month's dying fall, still

I shan't get home before the light has gone.
Over the Tay, clouds are lit up, wine-dark

over the hills, over the water. Still

welling nostalgia for the daylight drowns
all that worry. It's going as I look.
How long will our seasons' cycle last? Four

or five... miles on after the dark wood where
the bus turns – in the middle of nowhere

called Hazelton Crossroads – slyly my stride
starts to shrink, going home. My room's that far

horizon? Now light runs out on me, but
half-way there. Wellingtons slur on leafmould,
fudging the gun-shot rending through beech masts.
I fear it will be night before I'm there.

The Rose, the Hearth

1. *Corned-beef Legs*

When Felix kept on walking through the song,
catty kids called them corned-beef legs. They went
out with slippers, slopped between hearth and milk
left on the step, in watery sun. Old
open fires dying in electric dawn
down those mean streets... the bedsit lonely hearts
singe thighs. The good life's not chasing the sun

around the room... pussy-footing about
light stains over the carpet. Sun streaks red
beans in bags, heaped like some *objet trouvé*.
October oranges' and lemons' light
rings changes. Luxury's not chasing sun,
but being flush enough to crouch beside
the single bar's red glow. Calves blush, blotch puce
and cream. The meter tick's crinkled green-backs.
To warm the cockles of your heart, port wine
stain's dying varicose-veined legs. Poor Tom's
a-cold again, drawn to that blessèd bar,
rose at the hearth. Why does a fire console,
never mind how high's boosting background warmth
across the sunny – far – side of the street?

2. *The Rose, the Hearth*

They lay all night, on that mahogany
hall-stand, once polished so's to see yourself.
Rosaries of beads like tears or sweat came
beneath the cellophane, amid the rose
buds and fern fantasy... cruel April cut.
Bleeding moss roses sent her pink bedsit
with somebody's sharp weekend desire – she

didn't come on, until dropping by next
evening, tinged ashes of violet.
She'd not shrink from the next guy through the rose

coloured hot air, seeped like gossip from us
tenants' dirty bathroom, the belle's pump-room.
Her tone's another register for men
beyond the pale, and women. "We may not

know, we cannot tell" what's her cross, that each
must bear? Grasping possessiveness? What bar?
Bloody Marys and candles... they blew out to
vin rosé, spring lamb, sheep's eyes and nosegayed
self pleasing self, dear heart of all the world.
I took delivery, nursed that bouquet...
desired red roses, wreathed with flaming thorns.

Remembered Melon

"Not self-sufficient. God, I buy... glut fruit",
the hedgerows bleeding blackberries. The sting
lies in what's not said. Blankly gorged, like flies
on fruit, my eyes crawl off her white face, tack
across the Tay and grey March sky... Across

the carpet, splashy with blood oranges
and lemons of October light, *triste* shade,

a skiff of melon rind's veering away,
a paper tissue that white discard sail.
Pale memory dyes... London autumn, each
new year returning with a dying fall,
through *rosé* glasses: fly-blown honey dew.
A lemon melon bought from swift sky-blue
gloved hands, rush-houring through the street stall trash,
had even seemed a whole world in my hand,
gravid with what vague energy, in hopes?
London's people. All doors were open. Still,
across the carpet's surf of papers, books,
a melon skiff's ever my "ship of death",
high and dry. Blown back, heady scent exhumes
the yield of flesh as the knife hit home.

Tied Home

1. *Tied Home*

What price the view, a window on the mist?
Leaving again, I find I've left so many
passing homes, found and lost so many

rooms with a view, a prospect on the sure. At first,
through mist, the estuary was a landscape to be
lived, walking with a you. That ideal seen through, I
gathered November-mild December days
and the freckling sun, may... be life's little highs.

Going, almost the only thing that moved me still
was lodged in a corner, a copper beech leaf blown
half-way to powder. That never sullied the old order
"tweeny" maid's dusting down, before the ascendancy

of the mobile society. Leaving's nothing but
sweeping out, after making ready for the new broom
to sweep out any dead insects... the old room
taking in inmates, with their body scent.

2. *Tied Home*

What price the view, a window on the Tay?
the Dundee view, across the estuary to lush
and dun fields, as like as not mist in the frame
of ingrowing Virginia creeper, crimson sash. All lit up
with Spanish red and castellating sunset, at my farewell
party someone teased, "What would you give
for the view?" Only so many grand was someone's sure
fire line. Through the creeper's ring of fire, "the view's all..."
that kept me going through the job, the faces and
daze. Love's tricksy, simplistic ideal was
mist in the light of day, fresh summer. It's what wasn't
flowering... bound me there. Alone, you may grey with the black
comedy of the unloved? And now with the working of
absurdly human pathetic fallacy... another,
Perthshire field lights my eyes. Over the hedge,
bindweed will billow, whiter than white.

3. *Tied Home*

"Don't put down roots in a tied flat", the wise-
acres laid down. Still, the creeper goes on
insinuating tendrils through the woodwork... later leaves
dying, tindery. Once the books were coffined
in Tesco cardboard boxes, the room was wholly the view,
a prospect on the sure: the silting
estuary, Fife farmland beyond the mist... a study
in grey, framed by Virginia creeper's dying fall
about the pane, crimson with abandon. Stripped
of my evanescent personality, the room was
giving me back a sense of a self, meshed in
a memory that mayn't be true, moving in

with the mist... October day, years
to the day, the intention... A moth
was mazy at the pane, half-dead. My dry eyes turned
to Michaelmas daisies, clumped wine-dark
against the rain-green grass.

4. *Farm Cottage to View, near Gauldry*

Along by-roads' hilly miles, firs' slatted
sun and shade levelled my thoughts. I was set
right at one of their farms, whose yellow labrador
was just a wag. The arrival on foot is unlooked-for,
a talking-point at the big house, with the forebear
who "rode to St Andrews to post a letter
and washed the horse at the ford", before gracing the clerisy's
cobbles. A landed family's heir to a murky past, a place
in the sun: "a North Fife postcard view", on his working
capital. Beyond the glen's coverts, tiered trees rising
sap-green, still and dun... autumn quickened for me,
bare... gold. The quiet went without saying.
I coveted living there. Like a shot, the ground froze
symbolic and private. When all else fails, there's always
some place like this to rent, when you can work
making a pretty penny, buying a pretty view.

5. *Farm Cottage to View, near Gauldry*

Low to the ground on their rising ground,
the pair of farm cottages command
as fine a prospect as the big house,
looking to the trees' banked gold and duns.
I see them not through that day's high
wind's sun flash, but Dundee September's
rain slant from mist-clingy to good and hard
belabouring the soil... That day was my summer;
the landlord's poaching kestrel, flights of swallow.
I pined to live there, the place
moved me. At a loss, we're told, self

love is the beginning, making over, again, setting off
even an altruistic gene, according to our lights. The weed
underfoot's a face of the nature that fails only
impersonally, and cataclysmically elsewhere
while rain over a field lights my eyes.

6. *Electric Storm*

On such a night, in my ex-manse bedsit, I'm eternally
thankful for cell-thick walls between me and the gale
flailing October-drilled fields and half
field of standing rose-bay willowherb, seedy raggle
taggle, that was before my window. Since the walls were
raised, rain slurps there. *For the rain
it* fizzeth my thoughts, sloshed in their begging
bowl of bone. "And I, no longer I" am not climbing the hill
en route to night, spared minding sheep for time out of mind
to daub with words after the inner man, the soul of her
...spared living off land blacked by the gods
of another land, to outlive the brief life
expectancy of most of the world and all our yesterdays'
candle-power. A sheltered, near pseudo-life, I should judge
myself, at best badly ghosting an orphan of the storm not
...fuelled with food and fire, within tissue walls.

7. *Going Home*

In the outsider's insidiously grateful, romantic way,
I'm home when the *Stagecoach* bus inches out of
Perth: the neo-Georgian grid of neon
amber lights in autumn's rush-hour to
twilight. The hills recall me to returning to
the soil: turning dust to dust seems natural
in this sallow light, ethereally
greenery-yallery. Leaves dark as bark, elms silhouette
against lemon and olive. And deepest red in tooth and claw,
nature roots humanism. Antithetically, the sky's divine
fretwork to a religious cast of mind. I call to

mind an old friend's other-worldly turn to
whom this pastel above the neutral earth
colour's... would be proof of a life-expectancy beyond
"the good minute". Home, again. Errol church tower's limed
with faith's greenest azure, darkening dusk to dusk.

8. *Setting the World on Fire*

The light is going, ebbed away beyond
the tree-studded hedge straddling my window
and the builders' field of rose-bay willowherb, gone
over. But the elms still flower with the day's first light,
last light, and the clumps beyond are golden October. And
after the dark has drowned the lower branches,
tops of the trees are golden effluent. This is
the frequent, timeless scene they felt they'd

watch for ever. Even as I look... the light goes
greenery-yallery in the frame's shadow field.
I saw the shade go black. Jerking out of it, I switch on
the light. Work; sleep, finally. And again, dawn frosts
docks and nettles, willowherb's whirled
seed. With the rosy heater, on a neutral earth,
rise to a scenario like the last evening's melancholy green
and yellow, till the sun sets the fields on fire, again.

9. *Poor Tom's*

By my window, the tree's daily a scantier shower
of gold, stuck through with its own bare bones.
It's a November bobby-dazzler, attracting birds
to the end. Rose-bay willowherb blows beyond
gilding, dun and trailing clouds
of seed. I never fucked up anyone's one life, yet
I'm alone and coldly look about, don't see

behind the hedge a tit – great tit? Tom tit? –
will fall to an omniscient farm cat's nature, his
spring. This silver birch off-loading gold's an axis for
blackbird, thrush, tit and the eternal sparrow. "Feed
the wild birds in winter" was the message to his son, filmed
from a Teheran Embassy hostage. Love, be
loved, I believed, and render society a pennyworth
of reformist ardour, equalizing. Through sunlit fields,
silver frost threads among the gold.

10. *From the Window-seat*

Golden October, between rusty plum curtains, that must
...have been hung by the last "Wee Free" minister
in this ex-manse. Beams shaft the bare stairs, high-
light dust, fuzz in my eye. Here for the moment,
fondly I see through the orchard and autumn
roses, the mossed wall at the garden end. Over
the nearer fields, kids call. Beyond, the Sidlaws.

Over a gilded bed of rhubarb, half-way back to nature
an espaliered pear drapes a pane, stealing the day. Black-
birds peck at rosy apples, sour as cooking and surplus to
even the one-parent family. Or nuclear norm.
Where they fall, they deliquesce in soil. That must

...mean rich guilt for the poor, still with us
and without... In the sunset global village, with the less

blessed... how can we go on, more or less
in collusion with the system, from the first knowing bite?

Freeze

She seems a world away and looking through
the middle distance, as if seeing through
it all. And my Rosetta Stone skull, frost-
iced cake of brain. "Apathy'll see us out,
dying... through all life's strata." I nod, fall

silent. By night, alone, anaesthetized
my "good minute's" the sheerly instant drop
to sleep, into the black hole of that in-
most inner space. Through lulled subconsciousness,
you bypass at a nod all history's
interim glister on the sheet of snow,
dodos and the old fake sugar daddy. God
has always failed to come up with the goods

for cavemen cloistered in the dark night of
our souls, sandwiched between recurrent ice
ages. Humanity's left the big sleep
now. Dreams only forewarn if they wake you
hectoring, "Hell, you seem a world away"
lost in sky's no-man's-land of cold war planes.
After all, it's near criminal to want
to sleep now, with a present of the day.

Days of Grace

Why do all clichés boomerang...? "*You* live
a quiet life." "Not tuned to nature." "Who's?
whose? I shall never accord with mine, let
alone being... fine tuned to seasons' reel,
except alive to fear each gold-leaf fall
mayn't mature, through this last dark age. Peace
campers alone live our priority. First,

my last folly's finishing some work..." Lead
words ricochet over the uniform grey

sky, over the estuary. "But I couldn't
live so..." "Things lift the day. Some days are grey
minutiae clocking up a day. You don't
outlive your own imagining..." *No squall's
too loud to drown drowned Circe's call, some gull
the mind... sung up. In art, a mad king's songs
orchestrate life under the baton's hail
of hits. Mozart's a drug, stilling the buzz
of self doubt's muzak, nerve's fine tuning, far
out in the depths* "working... And aren't we all,
after our doubtful lights? Who'd not turn to
the task, lighter when some breeze lifts the day?"

Warp

Meaningless to ask what a city's like...
even the town of the three Js – jute, jam
and journalism – although lost for words. Hell –
I've lost her *spiel*'s thread "...the West End,
where they built their piles, after making them...
betraying their hands to the mills' treadmill.
Jam tomorrow? Pie in Tay sky, that frames

a Latin quarter now. The warm north May...
students in sweeping *dirndls*, bead ropes, chains,
drift between digs down streets whose names pre-date
the mills: Strawberry Bank, Shepherds Loan, Rose-
angle... that 'dear green place'. And all of the dole
kids drift really. And weren't we blessed to be
Supermac's kids – affluence fed welfare?
So lost out in private life, I should still
make something of this life, till shuffling off

immortal coil" – all's grist to self-accused
souls "...only connecting... loose threads like chains,
you have nothing to lose but... They shot that
Guy Burgess film in winter in Dundee –
City Square, Moscow. Half the snow was real."

Talking to Yourself

"*Grey* comedy's the name of the game." "What
game?" "Games people play. Life and death, the great
game, 'cos our perception of it all's skewed
like any swivel-eyed fly on the wall,
of course." "You're harsh now." "Life is, even where
full bellies nourish finer feelings, so-
called... 'modern love', luxuries like divorce,
suicide." At a stroke, she damns a state

letting her be. Along the world stage of
her window-sill's a blown fly, left for dead
last year. Light wings long flit, what's left will be

dust that's the watchmaker's shame – unique
structure. *We may not know, we cannot tell
how much it suffered there.* Idly, I muse,
"Why didn't dramatic irony go out

the window, when God died?" "On account Freud
showed us what the artists had." Why... has she changed,
am "I, no longer I"? With Eric's end...?
The angle of perception shifts "...with luck,
of course. If you don't sense the irony,
you miss the burden of my words. I'll stop?"

A Good Listener

Dead of winter, her wireless would be all
that's live here, with that eternally fast
clock, putting skids under time frozen time-

less. Then she's her old self, talking to her-
self? She shuns received opinions, yet
hears voices in her head, among the buzz

of good old books, plucked "thoughts from the air" of our
continuous present... she's running on
about. Now, that means picking up, despite
yourself, meanings beneath the speaker's words,
tuned to the other's thought. Illusion? "There's
no emotional equality." "No",
grim, I affirm "your first rejection", with
it seems many since... I fulfil my life

long side-kick role, always missed only by
default "...psychic wound throughout, deadening".
Once, May, Eric said I was born to be

"a good listener". I listen to her
abrasive home truths' rub: the salt of life...
tears... through my skull, that womb of echoes. Nod –
but when's my turn or am I crying now?

A Privileged Voice

"My skull's a psychic radio. Or bugged
by dying voices... 'shreds and patches', child-
hood's echo, fear. Wireless on, we've cried off
the real... imaginative leap, half hear

'You can't outlive your own...' colluding with
their cry, the burden of their lives. How live

in some state of but for the grace of – there
I go, running on to pluck... free thoughts
from the air, consumed by guilt, surviving... Yet
there's no emotional equality.
I'd kid myself if only I... I, I
too, could have had just my sliver of love,
my tranche of time, compared with lives of friends –
all of us richly favoured by world norm –
if he would've shared one roof, one year, a new
year's eve, spring, flaming... June and dying... fall,
I could have lived, a kind of cripple, bound
after the year's end to take up my bed
and walk back to lie... till the years end. Yet
what of the unloved cripple, with psychic wound
throughout, deadening written-off limbs' weight?"

Woman with a Mandolin

Half here, aching to see how to move on
from here, out on a limb, blocked, I see through

the air... *"Woman with a Mandolin?"* Plucked from
the air, words come, at a stroke. "I forget names,
the tone grabbed me." I read the picture through

the muted strain: things dawned through grey cells, heart-
felt. She's black full-face yet pale silhouette,
first and third persons whirled down, side by side.
She is the instrument she's playing on,
a plangent jangle. The keys turn in her head
to heartbreak silver chords, the golden bowl
of lyric... hand at belly, gut-strumming in

Cubist real time, mass reproduced. Sold on
the hyped-up sell, O *hypocrite lecteur*,
why must you prise the worker from the work?
And how tie flowing time's dimension down
on paper but serially, staved? In-
verse, in elegant geometry of lines
of thought, a mind's *vers libre* dying fall
counterpoints the other heart-beat drumming beat,
aching to come across to... anyone?

Portrait of a Lady

A thing of shreds and patches, her work table's
littered with odds and ends for recycled ends.
"How live the simple life with friends like mine,
day-tripping from St Andrews for the ride?
They bring their kids. They bring things – this jersey, shirt.
Beyond the just deserts of the Oxfam shop,
I'm so favoured. I back-pack most cast-offs there.
Who needs even a flea-market wardrobe
to dazzle bunny girls' whiter than white

powder-puffs, ape magpies' white tie and tails?"
Her navy jersey's U-neck slumps... drunk waist,
a gashed purple T-shirt heart on her heart:
shrimp of a girl, meshed in cable stitch. "And
still the automatic writing on my mind's
the shadow of adverts' sky-writing on..."
west blush-rose views. "Bar nature, nurture, chance...
we're free to affront our destiny, fail
safe primrose paths, spring... trip wires. So I slept
around at twenty after the light... that
failed, embraced celibacy. Ten years on?
Well, that's life..." freedom to have and to hold.

Weedy Plot

"I'll dig it, soon." Blown in, from worlds away

I eye the seed potatoes, rose-end up
on chitting-trays of Tesco-box cardboard:
Epicure, Kerr's Pink. Outside, under dark
sky... spurting weeds wildfire over the earth,
a struggle of loose ends against the dark.
"Once, Easter Monday was the day – farm hands
were free to plant their tatties", to raise flesh
white from *his* soil... "In daylight, last year's runt

will sprout, ready to plant." "The weakest don't
always go to the wall?" The tatty plot
will mould this year's staff of life, next year's seed
spuds. "Hand to mouth, I'll pig it" – grist to her
will. The 80s... free. "Blight?" "As you sow... high odds
you reap." The dream's wild... nature run half-wild

till "il faut cultiver notre jardin" for
real. "Some edible weeds. The plot was lush
green, going over when I came... lush. One
year's seeds leaves seven years' weeds": dandelion
salad and buttercups, trampled by the rose-
bay willowherb, the thistle's regal sway.

Reader's Friend

Hard, even in passing not to be... drawn
to spring's lush and dun fields through the wire-
crossed mist she calls the *haar*, though I didn't see

why... she threw things up to come pennypinch
here? In the end, Ann's more a closed book than
the Edinburgh manuscripts, my quarry. In
real life, who wants a "reader's friend", who is
for ever on the margin looking in?
With some displaced biographic intent
in my short time here, I glean insights in
to the other...? till the train vacuums me to
London, never a second thought but that
leaf turned. Yet, thoughts are wires trailed to the mist
– dear Eric gone? So all our lines... yet live,
fine-tuned, neural *vers libre* sensed like her

'82 letters' hint: "Never such light
headed courting of – damn all. So it was
only played up by my mind, over months,
his conversation? Sad to mis-read things
yet, sad failing to read... the old story." So
I construct an Ann out of throw-away.

Last Tango in Paisley

Passing shimmy
of frost and my light

steps twinkled over the asphalt,
over the cobbles... It was
a few days in winter,
and I was too

...old for children and too young to grey
or darkly guy

my wearisome propensity
to dance the light

fantastic! when I mis-read your letter,
flushed with a thought
of clarifying
conversations, making our way
down all our ways. To-
ward understanding, words
tender word. Under-

standing would be step by
step
     and I've learnt to mis-
trust instinct:
the lying tarns of dark eyes, "green
days in forests or blue" daze...

For all of a January week, starry
eyed beneath a star-crossed night, I floated
six inches above the iron ground, fleeced
...of a snowy shawl, protective
like skin. The man in

the moon turned on
my blood, hotly. It was the old
dream of talking through
...being understood,
so's to have
through the continuum of con-
tact with close on everyone

their sparkle, their points a-
cutely made, their life
thrust – a pair of

blue eyes. My eyes sparkled, too
brilliant, when I mis-
read your *au revoir*.
It is the old

Sub Rosa

Outside the college gate
the rhododendrons' riot,
imperial purple. Crimson and
the scarlets blazed away. Rose
...fuchsia... pinks and

cardinal purple. Golden
tongued, each floret: each
alma mater spells out
floreat, with all good

wishes. The botanical gardens,
cossetting exotica, became
the very image for learning's
fine flower. *A l'ombre de*... rose
trees, lilac time, remember

the white bloom of
rhododendron fallen to soil, wan
in the half-light under the shrubs
and trees, papery in the breeze;
and at the end of the day, rose
sky, over the hills and far
...the petalled heart, nursing
a tear.

Ann, before Lunch

I cup the mug she handed me, ten years
ago. Or quarter century? (Or nurse
is missing one elevenses' tea-cup?)
Outside, the wires write tellingly across
grey sky. I look back to what's passing... for

reality, that Coronation mug,
cracked. Was it so lined, cracked ten years ago

when in her cups she'd root about for cups,
for black Nescafé, after a hard day's
night talking down stars to London's late dawn,
through 7 o'clock milkman, the rush-hour's
eternal return of the day, down-town's
wild ragged robin skyline through the rain
cloud sky's sheet metal jags? Yet, the old days

mostly her visitors' sherry lit up
golden echoes against the leaden sky.
The vivid colours, they were there sometimes
not only for vivacious Ann but me,
lack-lustre self? Or must the past always
blow back... old summer's golden haze because
it was: at least, you *were*... younger then, no

matter what else... Yet, so old in youth, how
could I daydream the old daze back, again
for all that... gold light fallen on the stairs
making me high if I but stood and stared
across the yard, where dusty with the sun
"a tree grows in" Victoria? Gold light
lightened my step, a leaden echo to-

day. Yet, I was that damned leaden self at
Maud's Sunday lunches, too slow to speak, yet
not too slow to burn through straitjacket ice,
ultimately cracking more sharply than
any fishbone stuck in your dried-up throat.
As Middle Age banquet bones were chucked, at last
you learn the way to throw heredity

away, "over your shoulder goes..." Cook up
a self when it's too late! – hysterical
chat over her desserts, with the main dish

ducked. And what *was* there to say to Maud's stuffed
shirty celebrities – trawled from what deep
subconsciousness, their bon-bons of *bon mots*?
Ann was the life and soul of things, those days,

game to talk down, talk up every last guest,
view. Years later, I find her settled into
calms of intensively farmed North East Fife
– except when planes fall down almost, out of
grey sky she looks as if she's seeing through.
She sits by her sack of oats that will be
her... since we are what we eat. I still can't

understand why she threw up things to come
pennypinch here? To the end, Ann's a closed book
for all her slanted letters, looping their
loops: "...sad failing to read the old story. I
cared since I seemed to see my younger self
in him – twenty years older! I didn't see
him outside Oxfam meetings. Once, he drove

some jumble to my old flat, 'room with a view',
he smiled, like everyone. Never such
luck, missing the old 'calamity of love'
as much as ever you escape..." So there
she sits by her sack of oats that will be
her... since we are what we are, that's what we
eat. By the eternal back-drop of her books,

a tribesman tethered to his goat – "that's life",
she wrote – kids' snowman by the heap of snow
that's him, she is the sculpture in the block
sitting beside the block, porridge oat flakes,
cheapest of our whole food. "At least, we've not
swollen the population." "No", I nod,
at sea in the drift of confluent streams

of consciousness. Outside, the Tay tones in
to sky. She's talked about the rites of her
passage from Labour to Ecology,
"...inching to equality. Labour's missed
the boat. Survival. In the end, it's the same.
By global norms, we should be dead by now,
hugging an expectation of life, north-

aged." Now, I feel I am prepared to die,
equally. I've done what I could against
heredity to nurture some self, too
late. I shan't leave the world a better place
but two biographies, not noticed much.
And I'd my hard-won gift for perking up
social wallflowers, through all strata, through

setting at ease and hearing people talk,
except it seems Ann now! who scarcely needs
my spoon-feeding, choosing to keep her peace
or dialectically deafen me.
But what am I but some Nick Jenkins or
(first, third persons whirled down side by side), face-
less "reader's friend", effaced? It seems a life-

time back she said, "I'm going outside now,
for vegetables for lunch", as if her life
writing on Meredith froze real time, still.
"Given the time..." she'd looked to the white page,
the iced *gâteau* of stratified memory,
tongue round a wafer of madeleine cake.
Or will it come like this, 'twixt cup and lip,

the end, freezing us here like Pompeii
without a future raking up old bones?

By St Paul's Parish Church, Sketty

The evening's grey, and green and grey again.
Sweeping the grass, rain's given over to
the evening, grey and green. Daily, I skirt
the swollen spring. Tonight, bells scale the air
above the green hill's sodden emptiness
– silver torrents down muddy, bygone ways,
where blackbirds brazenly chime in.

Grey as a rock against the green, the grey,
the church hunches a kind of leaden grace
scaling the mind's eye, for some passers-by.
Bells wash over me, romantically,
closer to tears in midsummer's lush light.
They tempt with tongues of fire our mortal souls.
They tempt with tongues, promising the moon.

So, how irrational I like their noise,
these empty vessels, launched into the air.
Their siren voices... intimate to me
tonight is Thursday, with their practice hour's
amazing grace. Chestnut on green, a frond
for tail, an Irish wolfhound skims the grass.
Abounding grace. The sea is calm tonight,

and clear. The mist's the opium of the people,
rocking and shipwrecking our coracle minds
on images graven there, with our names.
There's none but the human heart weather-vaned
all over the shop, yet with reasons? Still,
none but the lonely heart, pace-making self...
I hurry home across the green, green grass.

Hugging the grey eminence of the hills
above the bay, the church nestles beneath
the higher hills, hills risen to the sky.
Eye can't go by the shaky structure, lost

in clouds. Behind a Gothic screen of firs,
the way beyond stays quiet as ever,
apart from Sunday's queue of worshippers'

Japanese saloons, chrome fig-leafed by leaves
blowing in the wind, the rushing mighty wind
across the wide skyscape of Swansea Bay.
Bonnets and boots get plastered in the fall.
Hell's keys are sycamore. Who sweeps a road,
as for by-laws, makes that and th' action fine.
Everyman can give tongue, too, to a piece

of her mind on our quality of life.
The church, these days, rises from its graveyard
with handfuls of cut flowers, compost soon.
Is Peter's rock Welsh disestablishment?
The church, these days, takes care of certain souls.
Don't they cross over green to bells, with scales
falling away, like this soil underfoot?

House on Mumbles Road
for Neville and Brenda Masterman

To avoid the flow of cars
roaring along the coast road,

stand off a little from
the pane. Framed, water comes

to the very wall. Yet
when the tide's out,
you can hardly see
sea merged with sky and the further

people are rocky specks
in a sea of sand. So

the bay expands
and contracts. Through this coal
black twilight, the steel furnaces flaring
over the water, at Port Talbot,
show up or aren't

– mist. One towering smoke-stack bleeds to-
night, holding a candle to
the love-light in some-

body's eye, guttering on. So
personality's perception
...the window on our world

overlooking the scene, so
you see through... rose-
coloured glass. Is every enterprise ultimately
to be shown up to be
built on sand, or lying

open to the spring tide? Ante-
diluvian, an accessory to Victorian plumbing,
the old wash-stand leans into
the bay window, peeling
ivory paint and spattered with sea

shells, pearly in my eyes and the light. Lost
in reflection... I'm so fond of
this roomy old home, hearth of lost causes,
where being English doesn't matter. Left

from the individualism
of Lloyd George's party, my friends'

tremulous book stacks in every room
dreaming... spired. Salted, their bleaching
terminal moraine tips

over their daughters' breezy 50s toys
and books, from *Noddy* to *Leviathan*.
Where's *News from Nowhere* vanished to? *The Power
and the Glory* and the rest of
Greene? When did that weathered barometer
last hazard a storm-warning? Whose
finger last triggered
the mechanical hand to intimate

closeness, signal sultriness
at the end of the long hot
summer? Last year's Flanders poppy lies on

a bamboo table, washed up
from the colonial hey-day
of *fin de siècle* life – an occasional

table, a litter

of daily surf. Beside me,
nailed to the wall, hangs
a pretty pretty water babies'
tableau – the Victorian conception
of children. The glass reflects the gilded, broken
glass surface of the waves. High tide

for Victoriana came
with the English

iron masters. In the sea-change of
their industry's flow and ebb,

this country's equally bled white
and transfused with

iron in the soul. When the tide's
at a low ebb, a steely sky's

reflected in gritty
tracts to the sea and sky.

Through the rickety sash window, shut in March,
the stream of traffic flashes
faster still. Brute
force fires our lemming progress,

going back beyond
our slither from the sea.

At the Hearth

Going home... you're always there,
after the heat of the day,
when the faces and images
at work would turn in
on me, enflaming

dreams. When *my* inner resources fail,
you're always switched on to give
comfort. Only
connect! When everything's black,
you go on going on

glowing. (Why do the flaming superlatives
sound so icily phoney?) Your warmth comforts
in the cold clear light of morning, cossetting
against the day at work, the heated
tones of certain colleagues, making
my blood run cold with their hothouse

back-chat. Loyal to the end, you'd
always be the same, even when I'm dead

beat – too weary with it all to crawl
to bed, only able to lie

at the hearth, dusty
with the ashes of a real fire,
still. After being so burnt, back

in the first flush of love,
and the next few flushes too
(weren't we all?), through
black comedy to the other

...hot flushes, there's no one
I know, holding a candle to

your constancy. Apart from
the itch in a couple
of early 70s

winters of discontent,
when the miners struck and hit
home with chill-
blained puce toes and you were a victim
of circumstance, in turn making me frigid,
you've always lit up, at a touch.

Thanks for the mutual
current between us, still

live though I'm past thirty. Dear
God... thanks for the fire at my hearth,
while I go on ramming

pieces of silver into the meter.

Iron in the Soul

"Iron thoughts sail out
at evening..." So wrote an old

favourite of mine, Lowry,
decades before his death. Black and
white, that sentence

melts in my mind again, sloppy
with the snows of yesteryear. My thoughts
fare backward, dull

six o'clock, after the daily drill
at the office. At the moment,
I'm near crying always... dear heart,

half-dead heart, down-beat to the end! Going
home, snow seeps away, over

the pavement cracks, where moss
would gather. "Les neiges d'antan",
in handfuls, flop from ever

sizzling telephone wires,
lines crossed on the slate

sky. All through the night,
Canada geese will honk staccato
over the Tay, over the two

bridges and the iron
ground. This early spring, first
light, they braille the night,
that clouded site of stars. They nail it.
Chilled to the bone and feeling
...stigmatized, I try to remember being

lovelorn's a luxury,
the icing on our northern cake, gilding
...like art? Here, in the city, we're blessed to feel

the weather only symbolically, apart from

a lightning death or two, each year. Hot
metal brands characters only

metaphorically... in the soft flesh.
And these days, reading drugs me
if the book's light enough
to escape, via a good read – a novel

life's look-alike –
anywhere out of this
world, this global village,
courtesy of Caxton's pre-

cursor line. So weepy acceptance seeps
from the snows of yesteryear, melting
at this gentle reader's pane. The image,
cast with the hot blood of yesterday's

passion, from a fount *autrefois*,
today reprints with photo-

setting: the dark reader's pane
mists "where breath most breathes,
even in the mouths of men." Characters burn

the page, again. I wrote a big name
yesterday, asking it to read poems to our club.
So I shove off my pillow a fat Penguin,
motivated by its maker for the lone
reader's identifying madly, guiltily.
Dutifully, I reread slim volumes:

an old favourite of mine, a decade or
so ago, in another neural life. Today,
he might look for a fee, far

beyond the likes of us. And why
do we have to see the man
himself, the bare bones of the bleeding
image – *who cares about a name?* When
all's said and done, he's not

like... some matinée idol, we're not aping
ravers, wishing upon a star. We read
his art, the marrow of
his work. How tellingly
he swings between the staves,
hung up on the cross of self and
hanging on for good. More

and more, I can't bear
reading on with you, unable but to feel

the spiked purple passages. Bare
bodkin clauses tear-
jerk, all unresolved into a total con-

text for this devastating
n-th version of the old world's
entropy. And '80, the future of

fame's questionable. After all, we're
told, we're all to be

"famous for ten minutes."
Falling stars... He's

spent... half a lifetime needling
England, his England with nicely

collocated *aperçus*
of such devastating point

apparently authentically amounting to
whoever's behind the wit, almost always biting
and bitter. And not-
withstanding the other

ego, soul, images of images, partial
perception blinding a mind
balanced by a natural bent,
the writer in me's left standing speechless a
while, while the cold reader weeps.

Pre-publication?

"Jim sounds like you." "*I* didn't walk out on
Metal Box, hole up in the Dales, the one-track
...Sunday writer, damned by a certain gift

of tongues. He writes me out of his racked day
dream: 'I'd sweated on finishing it, soon,
but fear of failing paralyses me.
Not flying, now... how can you work against
conviction of failure?'" How can she quote
his words by heart, so... ironic? "'...laid back
among the *literati* of earwigs,
chewing on mildewed newspapers. And fair,
the quick sentence's... returning to the soil.
I'm no *poète contumace* who'd make
it... new, ego-tripped through the groupie sheep,
fallen flat on your face to mouth: *the book*

I'll be through by summer's end' – which? – '*before
cranefly write fall across the wall.*'" "Maybe",

I whinge, "you shouldn't quote all this?" "Who says?
Isn't publicity what he's pining for,
the ultimate exposure... to the light

raillery of reviewers, and the rest?"

White Trash

"Delusions of enduring... fame through art
died with the century. *They're* so old hat",
Eric's 60s home truth plays back, through me,
that image... him, torn... off the cuff. "Yes, no
such vanity survived Hiroshima."

In indestructible yogurt cups, crammed on
book stacks, seeds greenly pinpoint the long day's
journey out of night... salad hybridized.
Books do furnish her room, and they are drunk

...stacks, leaning on each other's weak-spined backs
to teeter to the stars, the ceiling's flak
and fault lines. "Things are blessedly make-do-
and-mend – yogurt pots lifted from a Saint
Andrews dustbin." Ornament is the rust,
black-barred through pheasant feathers in a jar
like quills she'd magpied home, somewhere along
the line. "They say, in India, no scrap
of paper's blowing in the wind but is

scooped by some dab hand. That's why our fine art's
painted on cars *en route* to scrap, to beg
what price the global village, after all?"

Free Speech

"The French Communist ministers can't tell
where their nuclear deterrent points. Some smart
Brit journalist asked, 'But where's *the enemy*?'"
"True spirit of *Entente cordiale*!" Bat-
manned low over the slate Tay, some plane drowns
us out. A momentary roar rapes all.

"From RAF Leuchars. Their flight path lies
overhead." She'd out-stare the storm sky, grey
with life. Beside the firth, the winter wheat
spiked through the dark... "'All flesh is grass', in the end."
"In the food chain!" "We *should* be grass. Grass-fed...
beef robs the poor south."

"...Scotland's the old back door
to England." "*The Auld Alliance*'s *passé*
today?" "In France! Round here, I shouldn't wish
to say. My accent's wrong." "When shall we all
be coffee-coloured?" "What if – if their *enemy*
did come marching in, their souls going on
before?" "What of the Yanks...?" "'The *west* is red''s
not the worst case analogy. Where there's
some life there's hope, except for the earth's least... free
thinkers, dying to say you live by bread."

House Arrest

With food, my books... my life, a view... my life
being under sentence, for a year's less than
nothing, yet how long... will our seasons last?
Not in the cage, yet in a gilded cage
twined with crossed wires that intersect in each

of us, in me, doubtless, in them themselves,
with even blushing roses round the door,
my room's at last my Sabine farm through strong-
arm dictat. They riot in beds, wildfire
wars of the roses over hybrid trash –
the white, the red, all dying in the pink...
roses for roses in the *baas* face: fresh
wars of the roses, rambling thorns' barbed wire.
One day, a sole... pink emblem pallid like
your palm, and over night the spurting sprays
sag with new colour, trailing clouds of musk,
"everyone's wildrose?" In my dream, the rose

vied with the burning bougainvillaea,
cardinal purple, blazing scarlets... One
year, one hope, one May... one flowering, yet
how do we know we'll live till summer's end?

Letters

1. *The Snowplough*

I force the machine over blank white, inch
a metallic trail, slewing round the end of

lines. Writing you shouldn't be like writing... stone-
walling at every ambivalent word,
so's not to read like less than off the cuff
...the note? I stop typing: the snowplough still

clangs up the hill... a chainmail jingle-jangle
track. "I wanted to write you" as I'd talk
but words get in the way. The text's a type
of layer-cake *montage*: iced over mush
of slush, the road and soil, the way, earth's red

hot core. Do you write everyone so... kind?
And come the revolution, when we're good
to each other, how shall we know what lies
personally, sometimes, under a gentle
word? Under the eerie white light of dusk – June
midnight moonlight glimmering on the snow –
I goat-foot to the postbox in the wall,
iron-lipped above the snow's drift-line, so far.
Climb back. Thanks for the snowplough drivers' grind,
keeping open communication lines.

2. *Letters*

No news is always good news. After all,
no matter how belated the post van's
whining up the hill, it's the new dawn. Rushed
days, I'd leave letters on the floor all day
till blazing through frosted consciousness like
the ruddy sun, over the hills and far
away... The dead-pan thud through the mail-box
triggers a heart... sick lurch, daily. I fear
work mail and bills – their window envelopes,
a window on the world, with all the Day-
glo junk mail and motley factions of friends'
cinéma vérité, affirming they're
there, with lives. Red final accounts chill. And
in the end, even friends want replies – x words
tapped out... signals *that I* can't decode my-
self. The other day, shuffling the day's dealt pack,
I found I'd left your letter last, for sure
what you wrote would be said in sympathy.
Now, tearing the envelope's tearing a skin.
Like everyone with our liberal hopes,
so vulnerable, why then should we survive?

3. *Hospital*

Never the time and – place, even the same
damned country. I fret at geography,
for all the world a sick child with a yen
crumpling mapped mountains on a quaking sheet

of paper. Of course I write, eat, sleep – fits
and starts, sick of dragging about the place
...the undying ache. To walk's to plough through snow,
each chain-ganged foot a dead weight. Some faint air
of unreality mists lemon sun.
There aren't the names for early spring. The fall,
things going, we warm ourselves with Saint Luke's
Little Summer. Since real time was frozen here
some time ago, I wait your hand again
in the letters. What earthly use can be
concern burning over the hills and far
away, with fever with each day's post and
with nothing in the pile, blanched daze and fears
and fears? Reality's no paper-white
bandage on time, with things sewn up. In the end,
the hot gush of tenderness only seeds
self-pity: we're bound in time-space by self.

4. *Mourning*

Sky's uniform grey, black-braided by wires
like leading strings downhill into the mist,
that no-man's-land of day again, grey yet
survived. The chemistry of these cells, doubt-

less has transmuted in accord with all
the dark, the heart... sick lurch, the banging of
doors on conversations that will not be
held, with understanding that will not be

more than a dream? On sky's crossed wires' backdrop,
nothing's what it seems: flying molecules
penned by paper's *danse macabre*. He

doesn't write, of course. My grey mind works, of course,
looping the loop of hints... notes' lonesome trail
till silence staunch in the end or in in-

explicable falling off somewhere along
the line, through all the blankness of crossed lines.
Double entendre pins multiple truth in mist,
rain-lit and blowing like perception's flux:
veiled, morning reels greyly about... the missed.
What kills in art, as therapy, is just
...where is the poem, less the lyric flare?

5. *Local Anaesthetic*

The needle sews up nerves, like cobbled thread
through fustian gum. For the tongue, it prompts
an ice age between clanging peaks. While time
here is a snowy sheet needled by nerves,
my mind, laid back, weightless, dissects itself:
why don't bloody injections *freeze* these days
– this isn't hypnotism your mind rejects?
I wait for the drill to hit the nerve. Soon.
Through clinical ease, stainless... steeled and white,
I can't imagine to the power of
say, even five times worse. Five senses – live
nerves puppeteered by their electrodes, hands.
Don't you black out into the last ice age,
tortured? The long hot summers end. So dead
men tell no stories but survive to chill
our blood, anaesthetized by all their shocks.

The dentist swabs the pain, so my thoughts switch
back. *He* doesn't write. Time froze that nerve long
since... I think of him warmly, remember all

those liberal-talk contacts years ago:
friendship, never given a second thought.

In G Minor

"Yet remember that golden youth – the ice gobbled...
Eine kleine Nachtmusik scored, late, with
no note crossed through... nature's old profligate
grace." In the picture, the viola's laid
by... wine-dark velvet cushions. Horse-cabs beat
the aural fresco. Over the manuscript
paper, gilt-edged in candlelight's old warmth,
a trumpet dips – or horn, lent from a loud-

speaker? That record sleeve's His Master's Voice?
"Ever Mozart"? "I loved the irony,
ringing true. Now I only listen to
the up beat... if I can. Life, after all,
is all *adagio*." Her artist's eyes
bore into me. "The poet goes on down
beat to the end, trailing *vers libre*, weighted with
lead acceptance, while we, consuming... want
– the flare." Yet in our bones we can but doubt,
eye the old young Mozart with his wife, alone,
purely for warmth, dancing at home and whirled
closer death's door, in arctic Vienna
lacking the cost of coals and kindling...

At the Lights

"Mozart's the paradigm of *natural*
inequality, yet..." she fades to all
our liberal hopes. This room's not bugged. "Sure,
I still read history as Everyman's

long march", slower than the house-bound snail. "Too
slow for the individual, who falls

out of line." "By the way. The race goes on –"
"Apart from the exterminated ones."

"The human race?" To fill the gap yawned in
our idle talk, like waiting on traffic lights
again, I glance over their broken spines –
her drunk stacked books, all our green yesterdays,
amber Penguins from that brave new world, "pre-
war", feeding... mass literacy, near won
dream, here? "The odds were always against the people

sometimes winning through – Chartists, Suffragettes."
"CND, the Greens?" Along dusty shelves,
alive no doubt with small creatures like dust
hanging on for dear life, with long dead trees'

books... are her cups of lettuce seeds that'll be
fresh leaves of water, some more salad days?

Collusion

Consumed with doubt, half here... "A heretic,
you know, I can't buy much." I cower by
the miracle of the electric fire: "Enough
to live by..." "Good citizens spend, so keep

some of the brothers – and sisters – in work."
Second-hand, her rhetoric rucks the tat-
worked cushion at her back. She's leaning on
stacks of thumbed books' sheer heights. "Why must you be
Savonarola – roller-coastering
doom-watch?" "Colluding to the end," she mocks
"No doubt I'd freeze without the fire. The north...
all we lack's some third-world scourge..." I cold-foot
through her spate. Condensation clouds the glass,
drips sweat. Why do the voices come at me?

"...And *Meredith*?" "Slow work." "'Not till the fire
is dying in the grate...'" "Is life's critique
written off... Evelyn wrote me: 'I put
myself on the line, writing her... poor life,
luridly cheapened by my publisher.
Censorship in the west's run by the free

market. What price truth?'" "...That we can't afford."

Rape

"'Writing a life's near violence. I was

trespassing, as my sniffer-dog soul tailed
a singularly formed character, in

a word. I spelt out... blanked out pain in that

life, enveloped among the smoothed out sheets,
close scanned for any faintest trace of love

until her hand had started jerking down
the sheet, in tears, until at last she was

still, at a stroke. Through fine tissues of her

blanched words, I'd force the issue, stab my nib
– *check*. Who'd credit it? That dark lady's dyed

technicolour in this sensational
confection by my publisher. Truth's paid
lip service. Truth's a sacred cow served by
the bull market. This bundle of white lies and lies

screaming's not her... Only the author can't
abort a book, once hers. Her life. I loved

reading: old, broken-backed books spilt themselves
in light in my mind. Now I can't read. Truth?
A lifetime spent... seeking hers in that book
I want to burn. I want to burn my book.'"

Letters

This mild night like June, you would linger on
the road, falling away toward the Tay,
wide like a bay and branchy between clouds.
I drop letters in the walled postbox, turn
– one is a paper boat, tossed on the stream.
Beyond the lights' broken necklace cliché,
Errol across the Tay, years fall away
– London, Dover: *je ne regrette rien?* —
from heady springs, North Oxford gardens, nine-
teen's... flowering cherry. Almond? "The breath
of the night-wind" was bitter sweet. This white
spring, only the Post Office on the blink
– subject to Murphy's Law, like life? – held up
a letter. One of the ones that get away,
it drifted round the Borders, picking up

out of line postmarks in its own sweet way.
Like net curtains, the snow was blowing in
the wind... to lie like spring's winding sheet. To
"shutt up the storye" of the winter warmth,
I'd long laid by his other letters when
it showed up, weeks on. This mild night might be
July, the potatoes flowering, pale.

Silver-fish

In murky depths of sloppy consciousness,
we know they slither round the buckled spines
of out-of-date lives, weighty bodies of
odd matter long sea-changed, wise women's pearls
...silver-fish nibbling at the realms of gold,
utopias and Lyonesse. They browse
through good books. They live by the text: the word's
made flesh and dwells among us. And so flash
pieces of silver stuff the silver-tongued
dreaming a Golden Age, whose "poorest he
that is in England hath a life to live
as..." much as any Buddhist-blessed mayfly.
All interlinks. Silver-fish swallow lines
that jerked us up to marvel at the first

cause... that left us emergent from the slime
but able to perceive gold in the mud.
Nostalgie de la boue? Insects like this,
generically primitive, devour
the yellowed books that were a wood, a view:
everything interlinks, given names
for insects like fire-brat and silver-fish.

"The Realms of Gold"

"Rather quaint – your 70s fantasy
of long hot London summers!" "Memory's

sometimes the truth?" She'd turn a golden coin
of sherry in the glass, lighting up more

golden echoes against leaden... Fife sky.
"76 was hot, and my room was
awash with sun" flash-floods. And I, not I
then fixed for ever amber in his mind's
eye... was fixated over England's shires
that might have been the wine-dark sea between
us. Spindrift love! Poor sod! Why do we have
to live it all to learn? Reading drowns out
the watery "I", yet isn't the same
as life. Dyed in the light of day, gilt-edged,
the page frames war and peace. "That twilight zone,
Vauxhall Bridge Road's close." I *live* there. The past's
a foreign country, dream colonized and
cheats – "Who'd cry for Victoria?" Lead sky's

lead City pavement. "Shit, memory's self
editing", that's translating from the mud
of all our yesterdays, the gilded lie.

In the 70s

1. *In the 70s*

Under the warder eyes of tenements
all over town, forms of undress parade
themselves, airing forms of our fantasy.
But won't these pink and white limbs soon be dirt
specked by the atmosphere's smut, though we're clean

air zoned? Through rain cloud sky's sheet metal jags
the ragged robin skyline of down-town,

a stone's throw from Victoria. A rich
scent, olive-oil sun tan, wafts cruising flies:
it makes them high, then knocks them down and out.
Did spikenard, once expended, draw gnats to
Simon the leper's house and the abased god
head? Creepy-crawlies rouse the living flesh,
embalmed with dreams of *House & Garden* life

and young bronze gods. Dozy girls are laid out
mummified, once baptized in flaming June.
Why did Victorians leave "sun roofs", low
rear extensions of this-worldly homes, now
multi-occupied? Under my raised sash,
lie two night-shift and blowzy belles who mustn't
uncurl a toe beyond their rug or they're

nothing but pussies on a hot tin roof.
Turquoise-carapaced, one small beetle studs
a burning thigh, falls sheerly from this bluff
in our flat world, turned upside down, to spin
a shifty gem – her friend lunged, fails to grab.
Jade with a cut look flashes faster still
...while from the roof of our warm world, the sun

sparks in her off-white smile a Midas touch.
A ritual exacts sacrifice. But burnt,
even scarlet... tender extremities
would spoil the image – red-neck cheesecake plumped
down in the market, free for all the wasps...
The sleepers lie on till the thunder breaks,
calling us back across the sands of daze.

Reared sheer to one-time servants' rooms, the wall's
now snaked by fire-escapes. Sloughed, wrap-round skirts,
sweat shirts, spring sales' fresh discards, flare against

the drab surround, the sky, an air that seeps
out of lie-lows squeezed by the surplusage
of grilling girls with brief bikini briefs
and hothouse dreams of summer before last.

Sun, that frazzled noon office lime strip-lights,
from evening sherry's gold light transmutes
Burgundy red sky over the West End.
A breeze, tinctured with cooking-oil and sweat,
breathes from the swarming royal parks and lifts,
with flying ants, brown people homing from
the cut-price, supper round-up from back yards.

2. *End of Another Bank Holiday*

A golden hour of evening at home.
The stucco opposite sponges the light.
The cracked façade blushes for better days
else why's the rosy sky so bitter-sweet?
Last of the sun, tomorrow never comes...
In backwaters like this, London's still lulled
quieter than Sunday, with the mobile mass

ground to a standstill in long bottle necks.
Arterial roads snake to some bloody jam,
chrome glassy through the gold corn to the sea,
the sea! Out back, seeping dusk comes in in
gilded yards. The absentee landlord's mish-mash
of close shacked-up bedsits rears next door high-
fly mortgagees to the old system, the old

families. They've all gone into the sun.
Torsos stuck through each family saloon...
a many-headed monster, with the dog.
The leggy kids turn out teenage and race,
lemmings flash billboards mesmerize, and turn.
Do people still take shots and say "cheese", please
...whom would you con at the autumnal hearth?

Even down this dead end, you don't escape
the thundered passing of their cavalcade:
poor cousins of the tourists' Golden Horde,
out for a day off routine... day-tripping
gingerly into richly vouchsafed sun.
That elder god... darkly, we shall see through
idling engines' carbon monoxide fumes.

And when the first car homing in the mews
nuzzles this *cul-de-sac,* last week's rave hit
insinuates itself in my sun-daze
brown study. Blurring my page... it's the last
release: a tease that nags, croons, finding me
out on *champêtre* margins, half-gulled by
the easy stimulants, like blush-rose light.

...Some will not see the sun go down upon
motorway madness, litter of the drunks.
They comb the royal parks. Who'd pick me up?
No pennies in your cap to buy you daze!
And where have all the flower children gone?
Bare-foot, bare-faced, where do they drift dog days
with golden boy Mithras *en fête* again?

"Summer suns are glowing over land and
sea": Sunday school lyric covers up scorched
earth. Over the grass, under the oaks, cool kids
fall to dream under green leaves, soon gilt-edged.
Ah, how the *fino* light works wonders for
the run-down system, gilding frontages!
We broach fresh days as best we may, and long.

Tomorrow

Between the market-stalls pokes one of those
for whom life is the biggest sell-out, yet
"Hello, love" he catcalls, perhaps endears
if down and out he's kept a gentle tone
across the deep felt reaches of the night.
Around these nailed-down stalls, he pussyfoots
around some bird homing to room and bed.

She hurries with a steady pace and raced
heart-beat. Still, mid-70s London's safe
as houses... all lit up, her mind brims fear-
fully deep felt pity, seeing poor them
fetched up outside Victoria's front doors:
a foetal position, dreams anyone's
guess? Look, they only want what you've got, love,

a room, a bed, a door, shelter against
the dark. Perhaps life did cheat them from birth
or else they fucked things up, but wouldn't you,
given the million givens, the other's life
story, some tale told by an idiot
lolling among the market trash, sawdust
and tinsel... some home-bound snail's spoor. Ditched, dazed,

they stand outside shop windows looking in,
big orphan Annies with no happy end,
whose life was one long window-shop for whom-
ever would say they took the wrong turn through
bellyfuls of the dark night of the soul.
Only the hail for shrapnel now, for keeps!
Only the hail now, throwing stones at them!

Old soldier – vagrant – drunk and derelict –
tramp – tramp, limp from a hostel, just a step,
a stone's throw from Old Palace Yard: the House
of Commons does damn all for them. For years,

days, they hang out in sleazy entrances,
dead to their world's lifetime of stones for bread.
Whoever goes home, daily casts the first

stone. Huddled with the old bottle to hand
by night, by Woolworth's, by a warm air vent,
one watched the world and his blonde wife go by,
tap-tapping blindly, too far gone to be
hot in the shade of young girls' light and shade.
Younger, one night, one passing... self would've danced
home, with eyes full for whom love overflowed:

twinkled, twinkled little stars in her eyes.
He noticed, maybe... he can't see too well,
lapsed into pseudo-sleep and wheezing still
to hand that same old bottle draining hard,
till morning has broken and all the people
come with their purses, daydream realms of gold:
he'll have been moved on, with his present pong.

Tics and our winces synchronize like one
armed banditry gracing some trendy bar
– closed shop to them, for all the world... whom their
parade sauvage grossly offends: that's us...
the rest of us with something to our names,
something to bless ourselves with, even one
week's rent, respect in hand. And that's the key

to keeping your end up. Once down and out,
anyone hugs the drabbest shadows, peers
around bust, black plastic bags, spewing their
lot. Brain-washed, also, many women will
still thrill to see somehow an image has
caught on... the other's glad eye, though glazed with drink
or worse. So to the bitter end, they come

on role-playing, with a back-drop of stars.
What of the other... outsiders, all who

miss out on Sally Army care and all
who never had the chance to get to know
the dark recesses of old homes and all
who did? She battles with her fearful mind,
fretting to cloak low heels stiletto'd to

her room: that raped quietness. Safe home, she'll share
the good life of the other tenants in
the bloodshed of the film's shooting, below:
"Boots – boots – boots – boots – movin' up" to close down
again. She pities girlish old girls stooped
to kiss the news-reader "Goonight". Kiss my
– it will be warm inside: tea in the pot,

they only want what you have got. O.K.?
The gun-shot of a crashed bin lid recalls
the system: throw-it-away life-style. And
even Victoria's most run-down
consumer takes all in a wake of trash
– along the gutter, sprouts, even spuds. Green-eyed
in any puddle's mirror, see yourself:

don't look too close, but see yourself afresh:
you, you, you drab illusion in the glass
keeping your head above water, with luck,
and swallowing too much... plus the drink. You're
only another bundle of contradictions like
Anne, sister, like all the unmourned, like
them. Could you've made out better, then, dealt out

their lives' condition – inhuman – low-down?
High windows rattle in each tenement,
keeping each spinster from the probing world.
Here, dustbin-lid percussion's nothing but
cats' freaked-out sex, engendering nine lives
or slattern worse yowled through the twilight zones.
Some midnight folk think of the river, else

think they're *there*, but the bottle's not always
the old glad tidings of comfort and joy down
and up each alimentary canal,
along the tunnel to the ultimate
black-out. The journey to the end of night's
warmer across a cold bedsit than down
on the Embankment, cardboard against the cold,

the long day's journey, half a lifetime lapsed
when Big Ben hammers home the witching hour:
nightly, it's all the lonely hearts for whom
the bell tolls. Washed up under the penthouse,
the sad temp's like our pavement friends, apart
from shares in our society's life-blood,
bread. Only cash can keep walls round a bed.

So they lie low, these grey-beards in the dust,
puke streams of bright abuse against a world
that had it in for me – don't hear him out! –
choking on cider, throw up everything.
And in the end, for better or – worse luck
– the strong arm of our law will not lay off
chilblained old hands, picking a clown's puce nose,

a pocketful of holes, while on the skids
the wise world rushes past, as in the dark...
who can see round a childish mental block
preventing you...? Always the after-taste,
repeating on the past? A callow mind
sees sun splashing out pavement grey as gold
from mud. Older, it isn't, older again,

who knows? Damned stream of consciousness – may that
river run quickly unto journey's end!
They loiter, climbing out of hollow sleep
in catacombs of consciousness, that void,
like Stanley Spencer's resurrection hopes,

the men who marched away, who go without
...the mackintosh brigade, the ones we can't

stomach but in the end mayn't damn, must...
save from themselves. And us. As for the dead,
they've gone. We thank our lucky stars, but for
the grace of chance, *we* would be moved, that way
...part of the mass mobile society
they walked out on, back where it all began
and where tomorrow never came and all

our yesterdays blind-wall the road you fall
down on, after the feet pack up, call it
a day. Flat on my face again, who cares?
Who knows the flaming colours in a mind,
that greasy puddle, throwing up a self
against the grey, the pavement every day?
A panda car lunges into the night.

Sprout

"Come into the garden, Maeve." She sweet-talks
"pick sprouts for lunch", lush vitamins. So raw,
flushed from her cool eyrie room, blown out to
the tatty plot, snail-trailed by Fife's late frost,
I cower by the cell-thick wall. And shrug
my insulating Oxfam coat – a good
buy. *Not hungry but cold...* A far cry from

the old days... *bon mots* picked like bon-bons, brown rice
simmering on a stair in Camden, Rose-

mary's old sweetness, Madeleine, the host
tarted up with rough *rouge*... Sickness charm? – like
a severed Saint Christopher – chain hangs from

a car slid down this brae. Struck by the rush
she nods to – fumes. Sweet daylight gone, how shall
I make the train, twelve miles? What luck to be

waiting on lunch. *Dying from cold...* Across
the weedy plot, her blue green fingers pick
mini-cabbages. Monstrous hybrid, they're
cellular constructs of water, sunlight
fused with air helically round each heart,
genetically chained, in the one green globe.

Soil

"My God – tuppence!", thrown to the winds. My teeth
chatter "So?" Nobody's that poor these days

in the UK? "Cheap spuds are five pence a pound
if mine give out." *She* chose her life, lacks... "Give
the next-century archaeologists
a break." "If..." there are people to sift our soil

like the old New World scarecrows, gold-digging through
a rush of light to their heads, bloody but
bowed, bowed. Spreadeagled, her boot will soil the white

bag of blown Brussel sprouts, last year's last. Frost-
mauve, blood-flecked fingers flit beyond the pale

of parsnips or goodbyes at dusk. As if
rifling dust-heaps in Dickens' London, fog-
bound, the Beckettian figure must bite

the dust. Bent to the soil to scrabble there
after gold in the mud, the eternal way
of all flesh going to seed, out to grass

in the end we are... returning to the soil:
dust to dust, whose food chain links? As she scrapes,
I could puke. "Jesus. *Tuppence.*" "I can't stand

...wasting. Our damned society wastes the lot."

Street Collection (1979)

Even two coppers
contribute

a skeletal clink
against the tin, rattling round
against each other like two peas.

Gusts of rushing mighty wind
and traffic drown out
their brazen chiming in.
When we see the hungry, in the flesh,

they're on the box, again.
So it's true

the poor are always with us,
flickering on, in some corner

of the global village, "some corner
of a foreign field". Far away

passers-by with northern *embarras
de richesse* rifle the small change
of their inner lights and pockets

and skulls. *Fair
shares for all* beg
these little yellow

Oxfam lapel-stickers,
dispensed for your offering
to the old, beat-up

collecting tin. It's served
in many campaigns, for
the sake of developing

countries. The iron
timbre never drums up
enough silver and bronze. And
anyway, who wants

hand-outs? Some

down-market Twiggy, all
skin and bone, feeds
her apple-cheek toddler pennies
from heaven, to go on ramming
our thirty pieces of silver
against the tin's iron
lip. If two or

three are gathered together... bad-mouthing
the post-colonial government, will "people
of whom we know nothing" overflow

the street? On the other side,
when somebody dies,
some body's left
for street collection... Quickly

the tin's turning into a dead weight.
With a placard hung at the neck

like the last century's
charity child, I'm stood up
apart from the uniform motley
consumers, eaten up by
our lack of time.

Mostly, it's women who give,
including the slimmest possible

figure. Fewer men give
on average more, till

silver and bronze
weigh down the tin

and the shaking weakens.

Workcamp

Volunteers half-killed themselves
in post-war reconstruction
camps, in the cold

war, in the pre-*communitaire*
years before more Europeans
became good Europeans, richly
clubbable. Mid 60s, high
summer, it was the start
of a long hot summer, just
under the mountain
wherever we were, Bellay?
Vienne? near the greenwood's

slow fade. Slow burn
...beside the blown poppies, every-

body sweated it out, with bloody
tears of sweat, digging for victory
– peace for our time, for all

the time in the world. With hearts
at peace under a German heaven,
under a heavenly blue,
the sisters and brothers were busy
fraternizing. Fair girls axed
the undergrowth that had to go
before the light of day. I can't
remember what the hell
lay beyond the clearing. There's
always so much to do. We were
jeunesse dorée only on account

of sunlight, bronzing
in nature's free for all

the fittest... Only
in England would you dig a duckpond
at a funny farm. Poles washed up
there, in Gloucestershire, after the war,
all through the cold war, twenty years on,
never even had a psychiatrist
talking the same language.
Forty years on...? And the fewer

among us who could communicate
directly, the more international
it was, blowing in the wind
by every campfire. At crickets' midsummer
in Haute Savoie, on a bank whereon the wild
thyme blows... on St John's Eve
who leaps the fires tonight?
Not that randy Roman, butt for all
la dolce vita ribbing,
a fast worker with a pick-

axe. Or the red-neck, tongue-tied
Englishman, Scots in fact,
though nobody understood
in that blistered bunch
in that melting-pot. We dipped into

an *al fresco* bowl of gooey *fondue*
one moonshine night, *en fête* and fragrant
with rosemary. It stuck in my mind
with all the wild and woolly
work-a-day idealism of the young
at heart, with nothing to lose
but our lives. The harmony of
the Angelus or Internationale casts chains

through hands across the sea.
At an Italian lakeside miracle
of wine-dark water, *Ave*

atque vale means here today
and gone tomorrow... after
three weeks or months, digging
foundations for the road

to the orphanage or invalid chalets or what-
ever and always for peace, till
dusk's old glory of the red

sunset. Smoke gets in all our eyes,
blowing in the wind, yet
starry-eyed beneath a star-crossed sky
dewy-eyed youth, seeing
crystal-clear the smouldering conflagration,
sing up, sing up and sing the same:
"We'll keep a welcome in the hillsides,
in the vales."